守禮之邦

Photo by: **Sho K**
Osaka Japan
https://unsplash.com/@sho0316

Traditional Martial Artist

武芸者 **bugeisha**

Issue № 9 2021

Bugeisha Magazine, the world's favorite traditional martial arts magazine!

www.bugeisha.net

Issue Nº 9 2021   www.bugeisha.net

武芸者 **Traditional Martial Artist**
bugeisha

Contents

Seikichi Iha
Sensei

Features

Departments

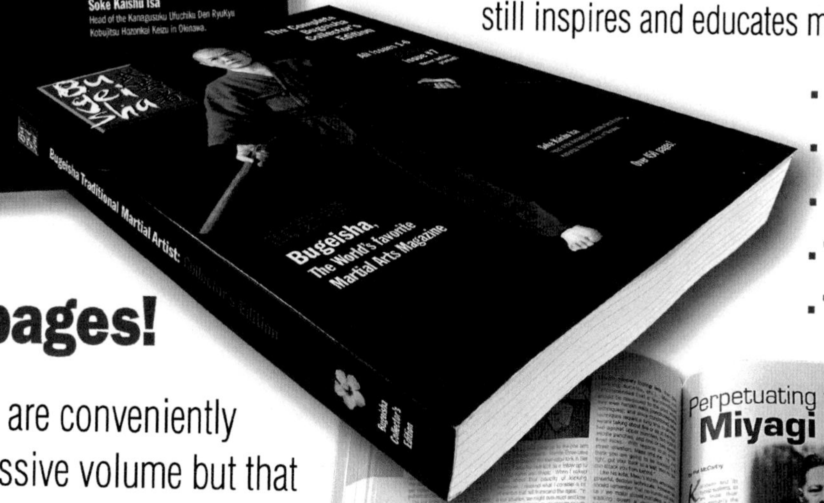

The Path
Thoughts from the Editor

武芸者 Traditional Martial Artist
bugeisha
Issue Nº 9 2021
www.bugeisha.net

Ichariba Choodee

An Okinawan proverb, which means
"although we met only once, even by chance, we are friends forever."

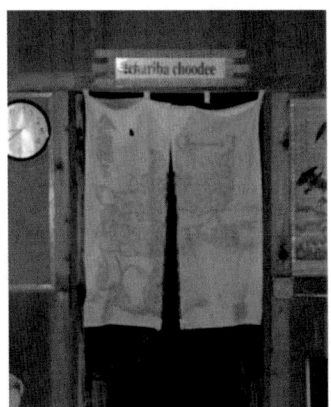

These are very special words that illustrate the friendly and welcoming nature of the Okinawan People. They are as true today as they were 100 or 1000 years ago. Most of us are connected because we practice Okinawan or other martial arts and we create bonds of friendship because of our common interests. Which is a little ironic because we are practicing arts that are meant to destroy and separate, yet at the same time can forge friendships that are stronger than blood ties in some cases.

The feedback from the first issue of Bugeisha has been tremendous! Many old friends have reached to me. Some whom I have not communicated with for many years, and I have made many new ones. Some are new readers of the magazine and some are new authors, but the amazing thing is through this spirit of Budo the friendship continues to expand, bringing us all closer together and not just close to home but across our world breaking cultural and language barriers.

This last year, where social distance has kept us apart because of the Covi19 epidemic, in some ways it has had a completely opposite effect. Such that there has been more contact (although virtual) via the many Zoom sessions we have all been participating in. I feel I have had much more contact with many friends and new acquaintances and seen them more frequently than before we were sequestered in our homes.

This spirit of friendship and participation has been growing even before the pandemic. Two years ago there was a Gathering in Pennsylvania where we had 5 different martial arts organizations training for a week under the same roof. There was true collaboration and camaraderie not just on the dojo floor but socially after all the day's training.

Later this year on October the Hands of Okinawan Seminar will be held showcasing over 12 presenters from different styles to promote and preserve their teachings in an atmosphere of friendship and not one of competition.

We have a growing need for connections and Bugeisha magazine is just one small factor in bringing us all closer together to share our stories, wisdom and knowledge, so if you read about someone in this magazine, follow the Okinawan proverb of "Ichariba Choodee", feel you have met him or her, and feel the connection, reach out, communicate, meet, share and train with each other. Life is short and preacious don't waste one minute.

Bugeisha features and promotes traditional Okinawan and Japanese martial arts methods, ways, and philosophy. It is a forum for promoting and educating the public in the techniques, history, culture, and trends in the world of authentic Okinawan and Japanese Budo/Bujutsu.

Bugeisha Staff

Executive Director
Editorial & Graphic Design
Angel Lemus

Copy Editing
Robert Wolfe

Technical Advisors
Bruno Ballardini
Nobu Kaji
James Walters

Language Consultant
Noriko Brewer
Nobu Kaji

Editorial Contributors

Bruno Ballardini
Chris Thomas
Donna Spicer
Franco Sanguinetti
Gerry Senese
Gus Albear
James Pankiewickz
James Walters
John Sells
Noah Legel
Marian Reitner
Marylin Fiero
Peter Ciecwierz Polander
Sergio Hernandez Beltran
Victor Amat
William Pizii

Contact:
inquiries@bugeisha.net

Produced by:
KOA·DIGITAL
Web · Print · Video

Kane'ohe, Hawai'i USA
info@koadigital.com | www.koadigital.com

Budo Library
Books for the Martial Artist's Library

This section features books for the traditional martial artist's library covering topics such as history, philosophy, and technical expertise in both empty hand and weapons arts.

An Old Man's Way: Doug Perry's Unlikely Journey Through Karate, War, and Life

by Jason Perry

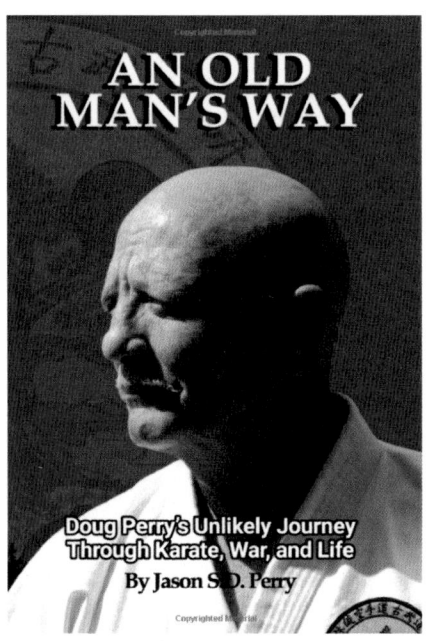

Raised by poor, adoptive parents in the American South, Doug Perry wasn't dealt the best of hands. His inauspicious upbringing from the mill districts of Charlotte, NC to the beach scene of coastal Carolina should have landed him in prison or an early grave. But Doug's course would be forever changed by two islands half a world apart. From Parris Island to the obscure Island of Okinawa, the warrior traditions of the United States Marine Corps and Karate-do revealed an unlikely path to self-discovery. He would become a highly decorated Marine and one of the most senior karate practitioners in American history. Influencing the lives of many karate enthusiasts, his path is a self-described "Old Man's Way," but old men were young once.

Available at Amazon.com and Lulu.com

Karate: Beneath the Surface

by Roy Kenneth Kamen

On the surface, Karate Kata is a collection of fighting techniques performed in a sequential dance-like order. Beneath the surface however, the Kata of Traditional Okinawan GoJu-Ryu Karate hold a secret.

This book explores a deeper purpose of the connective definition of the words "mind, body and spirit" and may leave you with the question of why the martial arts are referred to as an "art form" in the first place. The concept is life changing for the Karateka with an open mind and who is open to the endless possibilities that Kata holds.

Available at Amazon.com and www.roykamen.com/buy

The Martial Spirit Continues: The Journey Never Ends

by Marylin Fierro

The book will take the reader through many steps of growth and accomplishment through Martial arts as well as TV production and achieving goals. This is presented along with steps to help make your goals a reality. In the last part of the book, she takes the reader along with her to enjoy the journey to Okinawa representing both the United States and Isshinryu Karate. "Sensei has shown me that "The journey never ends", and that if you follow your dreams with a plan and keep taking one step after another on that journey, you will be able to do anything you put your heart to.

Available at Amazon.com

Okinawan Karate: A History of Styles and Masters: Vol 1: Shuri-te and Shorin-ryu

by Christopher M. Clarke

The most comprehensive and complete book on the origins of Okinawan Shuri-te and Shorin-ryu karate, with descriptions of the various branches, detailed biographies of the major Okinawan Shuri-te/Shorin-ryu masters from ancient times to today, analytical assessments of some of their accomplishments, and numerous photos and illustrations. This book is a "must-have" for all serious martial arts students.

Available at Amazon.com

Old School: Essays on Japanese Martial Traditions 2nd Expanded ed. Edition

by Ellis Amdur

Koryu, literally, 'old flow from the past, ' refers to Japanese martial traditions that predate the sweeping cultural changes that followed the Meiji Restoration of 1868. They generally have a very different character and tone from modern martial arts, such as kendo, judo or aikido which followed. More than the study of antique weapons, self-defense or a form of athletics, these martial traditions are a cultural legacy and a window to another time and place. In the first edition of Old School, Ellis Amdur, a renowned martial arts researcher, and himself an instructor in two different surviving koryu, gave readers a rare glimpse into feudal Japanese warrior arts, both as they were in the past and as they live on today.

Available at Amazon.com

Tales from the Western Generation: Untold Stories and Firsthand History from Karate's Golden Age

by Matthew Apsokardu

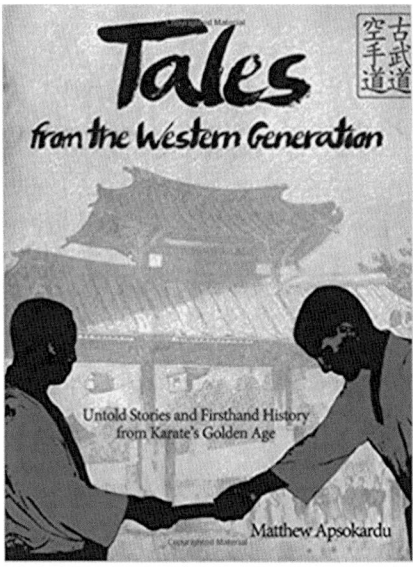

Have you ever wondered what it was like to study with the great masters of Okinawa, Japan, and the earliest pioneers in the United States?

This book contains over 30 extensive interviews with senior Western practitioners sharing rare stories, pictures, and philosophies. Also included is an overarching study of the history and happenings of early karate in Okinawa, Japan, and America.

Available at Amazon.com

Karate Archaeology

Raiders of the Lost Technique

By Bruno Ballardini

Comparative Analysis of the Kata A Methodological Approach

How to deal with research and produce something useful for the progress of the studies on ancient karate

After more than 60 years of folklore and myths spread at all levels in the world of martial arts, a production of high-quality historical research on ancient karate has finally begun, based on the few bibliographic sources available today. Publications of a certain scientific value are still very few, precisely because of the lack of secondary sources (the written ones) and primary sources (the witnesses, in our case the headmasters and their direct students who can report first-hand information). The main difficulty lies in the fact that the historical-technical apparatus of each school is still handed down orally and only internally within the schools themselves, and thus inaccessible to those who do not belong to the school. This is exactly what happened also to the Japanese, who learned only the most superficial part of Okinawan karate and thus gave birth to a totally different karate, disconnected from the original roots of the art. In this situation, many improvised scholars have produced—and continue to produce—very fanciful historical reconstructions based exclusively on personal impressions, without any real foundation. In a sense, we are still at year zero for academic studies in this field.

The purpose of this article, therefore, is to invite scholars who want to deal with this type of research to equip themselves with a more solid method to proceed correctly, in order to produce materials that do not claim to reveal absolute truths but that would provide other researchers with

Morio Higaonna Sensei in 2011 as a special guest at Wengongci White Crane School in Yongchun, China, executes the Tensho kata.

a firm basis on which to continue the same investigation, with subsequent updates. The method in use in the social sciences, those that are closest to this field of studies (such as ethnology and structural anthropology)[1], is mainly based on the search for similarities between apparently different "objects," on the verification of the sources that describe them, on the attempt to reconstruct the dynamics of diffusion of each object in order to compile a chronology of the antecedents, on

formulating hypotheses (always modifiable; this is of the utmost importance) that have at least a minimum of substance, and finally on sharing findings with other researchers. It's a little bit like climbing a mountain: In order to help others who are following the same path up the mountain, you should put your crampons in place only when you are sure you have found a solid foothold, otherwise you risk falling, dragging with you those who come after you.

Let's try to provide a methodological grid to proceed correctly, step by step, in this fascinating panorama still far to be fully explored.

An Example

In the following, we want to give an example of how a historical research on the origin and evolution of a kata can be developed. Our goal should never be to easily claim that two kata are "the same form", or that one has directly generated the other, because often between a model and another one there are centuries of difference and there is no absolute certainty even on the transmission until we find sources that concretely demonstrate what we are saying. The scientific approach is based instead on keeping all the possibilities open and continuing to verify which are the most solid or likely interpretations, on the basis of evidence.

Let's take for instance an historical kata like the *Tensho* (転掌) of Goju Ryu, which was created by Miyagi Chojun. While traveling in southern China, his master Higaonna Kanryo found inspiration to create his *Sanchin* kata by reworking it from the *Sam Chien* (三戦) of the White Crane. In 1915 Miyagi wanted to follow in Higaonna's footsteps and went to the Fujan province. Upon his return to

Kowloon Park, Hong Kong: A team of men practice the Siu Nim Tao of Wing Chun and demonstrate their skill.

Okinawa, around 1921, he developed his own kata, a "soft" version of Sanchin inspired by a Chinese form he had seen, called *Rokkishu* (六気手). A researcher of today would find here sufficient elements to try to identify the Chinese form that most closely matches the Tensho. And the most noticeable similarities are found in the *Siu Nim Tao* (小念頭) of the Wing Chun school. What immediately emerges from an analysis of the techniques and the structure of these katas? Many points in common should make researchers suspicious and should encourage them to pursue a more in-depth investigation:

1. Both forms use an "hourglass" stance. The Chinese form remains on the spot while the Okinawan form is developed on three steps. Perhaps Miyagi's choice was to create a "softer" version of Higaonna's three-step kata, so he implanted the arm movements of Rokkishu on the footwork of Sanchin (a hypothesis that must be verified).

2. Both forms remain front-facing in relation to the observation point and don't contain any change of direction.

3. Both forms contain very similar arm techniques, such as the crane-head block, the vertical knife-hand block, and the palm-heel downward block, presumably with the same function.

4. Both forms are executed slowly. In the Goju Ryu kata, forced breathing and dynamic tension have been introduced, but in some Wing Chun schools the same execution criteria are applied, albeit in a less forced way.

5. In both schools, some techniques contained in the two forms are used in the same way for training with a partner. So, there may be a historical connection between the *Chi Sau* of Wing Chun and the *Kakie* of Goju Ryu (therefore Miyagi did not import and elaborate only a kata but also a training method).

At this point, what can (and should) a researcher do? The first mistake that must be avoided is the classic one made by most improvised scholars: claiming, for example, that *"Tensho derives directly from Siu Nim Tao"*. From a methodological point of view, it's better to keep easy enthusiasms at bay and to aim instead at reconstructing a snapshot as realistic as possible of the Chinese form from which Miyagi Chojun elaborated the Tensho kata. Thus, a more correct goal would be to identify the archetypal form that constitutes the *origin*, and this requires some operations:

1. Search for similar forms in all the Okinawan schools and the previous Chinese traditions, to start a classification about this family of katas.

2. Compare and classify analogous forms by the number of repetitions of single techniques.

3. Compare and classify every single technique by similar applications in different schools.

4. Compare the family trees of each tradition to see if there was any possible transmission of techniques from one stream to another.

5. Verify as far as possible the periods in which the headmasters who handed down a different version of the same kata had exchanges with other masters, and of which school.

6. Verify what modifications were introduced on the original Chinese techniques, in what period, and according to what technical interpretation or Okinawan tradition.

This approach is valid for all the historical Okinawan kata. The parameters to be compared or verified can be many more, and all this work should finally implement a historical-technical database that would allow establishing with an acceptable approximation of all the paths of diffusion of a single technique or kata between China and Okinawa. It would be wrong, however, to force the research to identify, for example, a common basic template on which the Chinese and Okinawan schools have merely made some variations, because here the transition from one geographical area to another, from one school to another, would involve centuries of difference, and not a few decades as usually happens in the case of variations made by students belonging to the same family tree or the same school and in the same geographical area. Conversely, one can also try to identify a basic, common template (what could be called the X template), among the various existing versions of the same kata, within the same school, or among masters who studied with the same schoolmaster, always keeping in mind that the schoolmaster may have taught different versions of the same kata in different periods of his life based on the applications he was studying for his practice.[2]

This difficult and meticulous work will help correct fundamental errors in the historiography of karate, errors into which even 20th-century masters such as Funakoshi Gichin himself fell, creating immense confusion when, for example, he classified the kata according to the *Shorin* and *Shorei* categories, which never existed. This confusion has only recently been clarified by conscientious researchers such as Mario McKenna, who has not failed to emphasize Funakoshi's initial good intentions. Unfortunately, Funakoshi was not equipped with a correct historiographical method and was therefore forced to invent empirical categories that were not even in use in Okinawa, contradicting himself several times in his writings.[3] This should make us understand that good historical research must necessarily proceed in small steps, with continuous verifications, and without giving discounts to anyone.

We are still far from having people like Marcel Mauss, Claude Levi-Strauss, or Kurt Sachs in the field of research on martial arts and in particular on ancient karate. There is a lot of work to be done, and we wish for the birth of a new generation of researchers who do not limit themselves to finding what anyone can find on the net, and on the other hand do not rely only on secondary written sources (for example the English texts of other scholars or English translations of oriental texts, taken as they are without verifying them), but rather go in, first-person, in search of the last elderly heirs of the schools, to get first-hand information from them, and go in search of original unpublished texts and translate them, and use a scientific method in their analysis as ethnologists, historians, and anthropologists have always done. It is a difficult road, but unfortunately, there is no other way to get closer to the truth and dispel the ridiculous legends that still circulate in our world. ☉

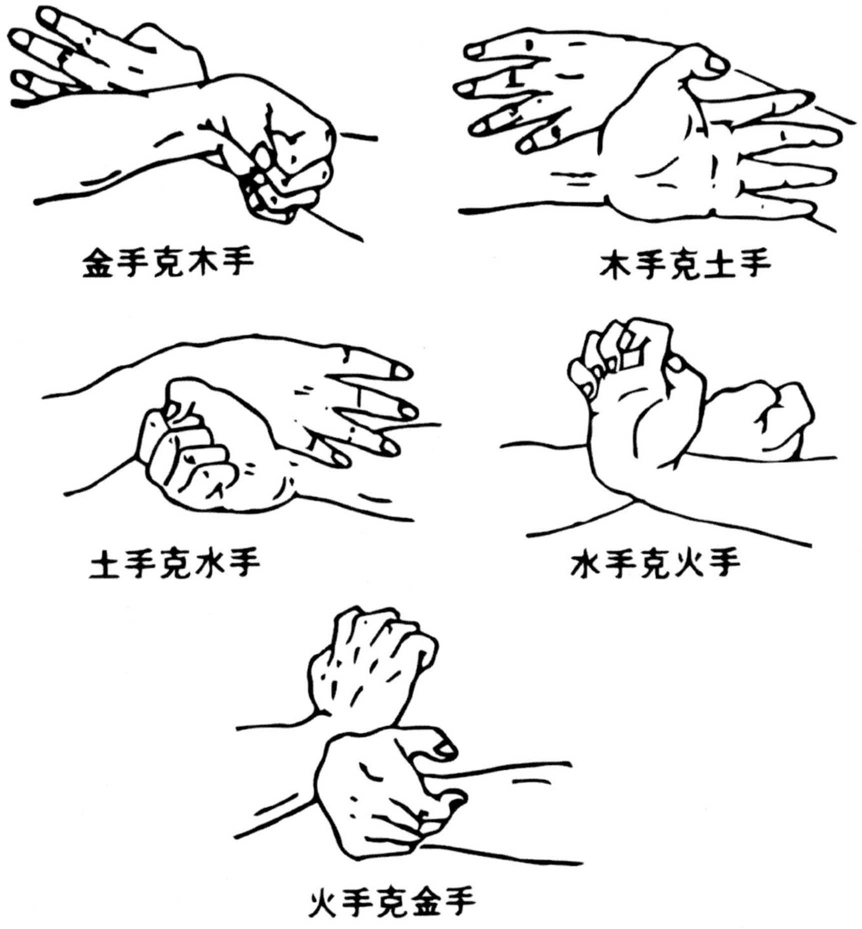

金手克木手

木手克土手

土手克水手

水手克火手

火手克金手

Beware of easy interpretations. Many people mistake this drawing as a graphic representation of the mythical Rokkishu. But instead this is the Five Element Technique of Tiger Boxing. Three of these combinations survive in Wing Chun's *Chi Sau* while they have totally disappeared in Goju Ryu's *Kakie*. The cycle of the elements should be read like this:

jīn shǒu 金手 (metal hand) ke 克 (overcomes)
mù shǒu 木手 (wood hand) ke 克 (overcomes)
tǔ shǒu 土手 (earth hand) ke 克 (overcomes)
shuǐ shǒu 水手 (water hand) ke 克 (overcomes)
huǒ shǒu 火手 (fire hand) ke 克 (overcomes)
jīn shǒu 金手 (metal hand) starting the cycle over.

Notes

[1] Epistemology today establishes different criteria of *scientificity* among the sciences. Humanistic sciences such as sociology, cultural anthropology, ethnology, which are closer to our field of investigation, cannot use the same methodological criteria as nuclear physics or mathematics, but they can reach a reasonable, "scientific" honesty by using their own verified and consolidated method.

[2] Example: In Kyan Chotoku's school there are noticeable differences between the kata taught by the two main direct students, Shimabukuro Zenryo and Nakazato Joen, and yet both headmasters claimed not to have made any changes to the katas.

[3] Mario McKenna, Okinawa Kata Classification, An Historical Overview, *Classical Fighting Arts*, Issue No. 1 (2003), pp. 18–26.

Author Information

Bruno Ballardini - European Director International Shorinjiryu Zentokukai Tode
brunoballardini.bb@gmail.com
www.zentokukai.com

Kyan-Ha Karate

Oyakata Kobujitsu

Hombu Dojo Miami, Florida

International Zentokukai Tode Association

The Zentokukai is an Okinawan Karate (Tode) Association founded in 1997 by Tim Rodgers, Angel Lemus, Jim Pizii and Walter Dailey. Dedicated towards the preservation of the old ways and the teachings of Chotoku Kyan and Zenryo Shimabukuro.

Tim Rodgers
President
Miami, Fl USA

Angel Lemus
Vice-President
Kaneohe, HI USA

Jim Pizii
Secretary
West Chester, PA USA

Larry Hall
Councilor
Quartzite AZ USA
Zenshu-Ha

Bruno Ballardini
Europe Director
Rome, Italy

◆ **Shorin-ji Ryu Karate**
Sukunaihayashi Shorin-Ryu

◆ **Oyakata Kobujitsu**

◆ **Kojo Ryu Karate**
Okinawa's Ghost Style

◆ **Non Sports Karate**

Chotoku Kyan

In Memory

Walter Dailey
Hanshi 10th Dan
Zenshu-Ha

Co-founder of
Zentokukai

The Zentokukai has Dojos in the USA, Colombia, Italy, France and Germany
www.zentokukai.com

Martial Insights

By John Sells

Impressions From Experience

You Say Dai, I Say Sho!

First in a Series on Historically Common Terms Used in Karate Kata Names

Recently, I was reviewing kata for a long-time student. Kata, "forms," are the ubiquitous and traditional stylized training routines of karate, ideally handed down from teacher to student—each style with its own unique set. At one time, kata seems to have been the primary skill-building method of the art, aside from a few specialized fighting techniques, knuckle conditioning, and weapons training. My student is also an experienced instructor, so the questions that arise are usually very challenging. I was asked about why certain kata are called dai and sho, when they otherwise have the same name.

NOTE: In the old Ryukyukuan dialect of Okinawa, Dai and Sho are expressed as Taachi and Teechi.

I started talking about the image of the *daisho*, the pair of swords worn by samurai before the modern era, consisting of a "big," primary sword—the *katana*—and a "small," or secondary blade—*wakizashi*—and how the "sho" version of a kata was originally thought of as shorter than the "dai" version. But then I was tripped up, because this student reminded me of the Shotokan forms called *Gojushiho Dai* and *Gojushiho Sho* (whichever one, depending on the group nowadays, is called *Dai* or *Sho*!). Also, what about the Kotaka-ha Shito-ryu *Shihokosokun Dai and Shihokosokun Sho*? And, by the way, the Okinawan Shorin-ryu (Chibana type) kata called *Passai Dai* and *Passai Sho*? How can you tell which one is bigger and which is actually smaller? Okay, okay, says I. Maybe I need to think about this, because there isn't a brief, one-size-fits-all answer. It's obvious, from even casual observation, that it must have more to

do with the origin of the forms in question—at least nowadays—and less with their actual length.

This got me thinking about Chuzo Kotaka's *Shihokosokun Sho* kata, because Kotaka Sensei devised this

> **Shuri, Naha, and Tomari are now (along with other villages) all part of the mega-city of Greater Naha, though they were once separate districts.**

kata in the very early 1970s as a companion to the commonly practiced Shito-ryu form, *Shihokosokun*. It was Kotaka who, moving to Hawaii from Japan with the American, David Krieger, launched his Kotaka-ha Shito-ryu group under the banner of the International Karate Federation, branching out from the Motobu-ha Shito-ryu Karatedo. The *Shihokosokun Sho* form was based on the other commonly practiced form, *Kosokun Sho*, but with *Shihokosokun Sho*, as with *Shihokosokun*, the line of movement (*embusen*) was mostly side-to-side. No matter that *Shihokosokun Sho* was most definitely NOT shorter or smaller than *Shihokosokun*; those of us who learned and practiced loved its long, solid, and unambiguously *Shurite* type technique. Of course, this meant that

henceforth, the original *Shihokosokun* would be known in Kotaka-ha Shito-ryu as *Shihokosokun Dai.* It did not mean that everyone or group who practiced the single *Shihokosokun* pattern changed, or should change, their kata to *Shihokosokun Dai*. Clearly, why should they, or anyone else, even care, or have to care? It should be evident that the development and use of this *Shihokosokun* kata, had and does not have anything to do with anyone outside of the Kotaka-ha system, unless they chose or choose to adopt the *Shihokosokun Sho* for their own study and practice. It's also worth noting, that there are other forms in Kotaka-ha with *Dai* and *Sho* appellations, not found in other systems.

Even if adopted by people outside of the Kotaka-ha system who also currently practice the "original" *Shihokosokun* kata, that doesn't mean, nor follow, that they should adopt the "dai" appellation for their own *Shihokosokun* kata. There is precedent in current karate custom for using the *dai* or *sho* term on one kata, but not the other with the same name. To wit: *Ohan Dai* and *Anan Dai* in Okinawan Ryeui-ryu are included in the syllabus and practiced alongside just plain *Ohan* and *Anan*. There is no *Ohan Sho* or *Anan Sho*. More examples of this nomenclature practice are bound to develop as the arrow of time moves inexorably on in only one, unfolding direction in the spacetime of our existence, never backward. One that comes to mind is the recently created *Suparinpei Sho*, that actually is shorter, by a lot, than the original *Suparinpei*—a kata used mostly in Goju-ryu and Shito-ryu, but because of the proliferation of modern

A youngish Chuzo Kotaka, founder of Kotakaha Shito-ryu, and a younger John Sells, circa 1975. Kotaka Sensei added to the corpus of the dai and sho kata terminology with kata of his own development.

"traditionalistic style" tournament karate, its practice has spread.

But what about the earlier examples of *dai* and *sho* pairs in Okinawan and Japanese mainland-originated styles? How do they compare with the above Shito-ryu example, as used within the respective styles, or to similar pairs, using what amounts to the same name and pattern, in separate, disparate styles? In Okinawan Shorin-ryu groups that descend from the teachings of Choshin Chibana, you will find the kata *Passai Dai* and *Passai Sho*. You will also find *Kusanku Dai* and *Kusanku Sho*. The *Kusanku* forms correspond to the *Kanku* kata in Shotokan and to certain *"Kushanku"* kata in some other styles, as well as to the *Kosokun Dai* and *Sho* in Shito-ryu

(and derivatives) and some schools descended from Kanken Toyama of the Shudokan Karatedo, a contemporary of the founders of Shito-ryu, Shotokan, and Choshin Chibana.

In the main, the *dai* and *sho* forms of *Kusanku* in "Chibana Shorin-ryu" correspond directly to the *Kosokun Dai* and *Kosokun Sho* of Shito-ryu, and other derivative styles. Why? Because these systems share an ultimate derivation from Anko Itosu (1833–1915), often cited as the font of Shurite/Shorin-ryu. Same origins, same kata, right? But hold on, not all styles having kata using those same names correspond so neatly to the patterns of the above. Some Japanese Gensei-ryu groups, for example, also

practice kata called *Koshokun Dai* and *Sho*, but they are distinctly different from the aforementioned forms. Of course, Gensei-ryu ultimately traces its origins to somebody other than Itosu, yet the names and terminology are the same. And, by the way, there's no value added in getting hung up on whether to pronounce or spell these names as *Kushanku, Kusanku, Kosokun or Koshokun*. I remember Ryusho Sakagami, who personally knew the founders of Shito-ryu, Shotokan, and some Shorin-ryu and Okinawan Weaponry organizations, in his Tsurumi dojo in Yokohama, Japan, writing over on the page in his book, *Karatedo Kata Taikan,* (that he gifted to some foreign students), introducing the *Kosokun* forms, in thick black cursive English style script: "Kusanku."

As for *Passai Dai* and *Sho*, forms that are very commonly practiced throughout the karate world, what's known as *Passai Dai* in "Chibana Shorin-ryu" corresponds to a completely different pattern than the equivalently named kata in *Bassai* Shito-ryu and Shotokan. In Shito-ryu and even in some Shorin-ryu groups in mainland Japan, the Chibana *Passai Dai* is exactly the same kata that's called *"Matsumura Bassai."* It's also sometimes referred to as *Tawada Passai/Bassai* (from Matsumura's student, Tawada), both by Okinawan and mainland groups. Whether Matsumura Sokon (1808–1899, according to his tombstone) actually practiced and taught this exact kata in this precise way is a different question, but that's what it's called.

The Chibana Shorin-ryu *Passai Sho* is the same pattern practiced as *Bassai Dai* in Shito-ryu, Shotokan, and others in Japan. However, the form known as *Bassai Sho* in Shito-ryu and Shotokan, et al., is practiced as *Koryu Passai* in Chibana Shorin-ryu and those groups who adopted Chibana's *Passai* forms. (More about the historical use and abuse of the term *Koryu* at another time.) Supposedly, these kata are part of the historical stream of karate generally called *Shurite* (from the Okinawa or "Ryukyu" king's home, *Shuri*), leading back through Itosu to Matsumura and thence to someone remembered as *Tode ("Karate")* Sakugawa (most likely the Sakugawa who died in the 1840s, not 1815, as shown on endless karate lineage charts).

But, hold on, the earliest extant

historical references to Itosu are by Anko Asato (a student of Matsumura), and Gichin Funakoshi (Asato's student). And they clearly say that Itosu's instructors were "Gusukuma" (of Tomari?) and "Nagahama" (now *Nakaima*—the family that formalized the modern karate style of Ryuei-ryu). In later writings, Funakoshi even talks about training briefly with Matsumura, seemingly without actually linking Itosu to Matsumura. To complicate matters further, if you look at the practice of Okinawan Matsumura Shorin-ryu karate, their forms known as *Passai Dai* and *Sho* (members of that style seem to prefer to pronounce it *Pai-sai*) differ in many ways from all the above. To be sure, you can certainly unpick most of this if you care enough to really dive deeply into the details of technique and development over time, following the trails of individuals. But that's a story for another time.

Note: Shuri, Naha, and Tomari are now (along with other villages) all part of the mega-city of Greater Naha, though they were once separate districts. The distinctions between the karate from each of these areas were probably not recognized or acknowledged until the early twentieth century.

So, what does all this mean? Because it seems apparent—even obvious—that oftentimes the terms *Dai* and *Sho* are appended arbitrarily without regard to which is shorter or longer, instead of using the numerical 1, 2, 3, etc., simply to distinguish one form from another. Historically, such terms were in use at least as far back as 100 years ago. Choki Motobu, a karate personage of some renown in the early twentieth century mentions in his 1926 book, *Okinawa Kempo Karatejutsu on Kumite*, the forms *Passai Dai* and *Sho, Kusanku Dai* and *Sho*. In the 1930 Book, *Kempo Gaisetsu,* by Miki and Takada, *Bassai Sho* and *Kushanku Sho* are listed and illustrated.

It may be possible you will never need to deal with what *Dai* and *Sho* mean in kata names—and there are styles and factions without such kata. Realistically however, in this era of information overkill, that's hardly

likely. If you're involved in teaching karate, you'll probably need to explain or at least talk about this issue of terminology at some time or another. Unfortunately, if you're a student who doesn't or may never teach karate, just be aware that people of all ranks and experience have been known to argue over which kata is or should be called "*sho*" or "*dai*," as they do over many other things. Even to the point of wasting so much time, that any reason to care is lost.

Don't be surprised if these arguments seem like you've fallen into a universe where you can hear—no matter what you do—the 1930s RKO movie studio dance team of Ginger Rogers and Fred Astaire singing that "*you say pa-tay-toe, and I say pa-tah-toe,*" show-tune in an endless loop. Worse still, it reinforces an environment where internet bullying is endemic; where people hide behind the world wide web, ready to lash out at anything or anybody that doesn't fit whatever mental model, orthodoxy, or fantasy they've adopted. Sometimes though, it's obviously for commercial reasons, clearly because someone has a vested interest in the karate information they're peddling as "the real stuff." Give it a rest, I say. Indeed, how does this behavior fit in with the lofty words found in so many prominently displayed and chanted "Precepts of the Dojo" (*Dojo Kun*) found on the walls of most traditional karate training spaces? Bottom line, if it doesn't apply to you directly, why care?

Note: Future "Martial Insights" will discuss, 1) The use and application of the term Koryu; and, 2) The practice of using Okinawan/Japanese personal and place names as kata-name prefixes.

Author Information

John Sells is a long time karate and allied martial arts practitioner. He has earned black belt ranking in several styles of karate including Kojo-ryu and Ryuei-ryu, including the Hanshi award given in Seito Shito-ryu by Kenzo Mabuni. He is the author of a general history of karate called "Unante-The Secrets of Karate." Currently, he is working on an historical novel set in the early Dark Ages of post Roman Britain.

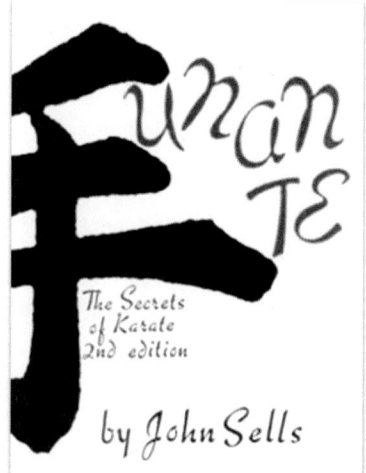

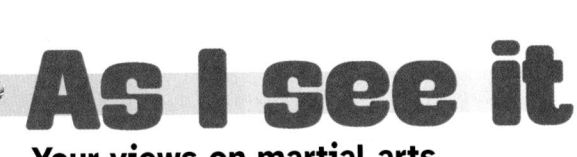

As I see it
Your views on martial arts

By William Pizii

How Okinawan Karate Helped Me in Sports

I studied Shorinjyu Ryu for about twelve years. At age sixteen, my hobbies shifted and I decided to pursue my high school sports with more focus, and I ended my training. While I trained and played Soccer and still actively compete in the Javelin Throw today, the lessons I learned during my formative years in the martial arts aided me in my athletic journey.

It is easy to point out how martial arts helped my time in soccer. Yes, those years of roundhouse kicks helped establish a sufficient volley when the ball was in the air, but, of the two, it improved my understanding of throwing to much larger degree.

Javelin and martial arts have a similar cadence. We practice our katas, bunkai, and isolated drills to a different speed than what they are applied to: self-defense. The javelin throw works the same way. We train at slower speeds, and when the time comes it all seems to come out in a ballistic, powerful manner.

Practicing katas and its bunkai helped me compartmentalize the different techniques in javelin, and it allowed me to pursue the deeper meaning behind the positions that I must get into. I learned the "why" question from martial arts.

An example that directly translates from one to the other is the hip rotation. Take a simple punch from a front stance (Zenkutsu Dachi) or square stance (Shiko Dachi). When we go to punch, our hip leads the punch; it initiates the action. By rotating the hip, we move our weight forward from our back leg to our front leg, and that weight shift will translate into the punch. By the end of the punch, the hip extends and gives the arm farther reach. The hip rotation in the javelin throw is exactly the same. The only difference is the arm placement. Once the weight shifts and the hip rotates, the arm goes. The power and speed come from our legs, through our hips,

Karate reverse punch with hip rotation

which release the arm. It's a reaction.

Finally, I must talk about kata and its applications. Each move in a kata has a story. In many cases, it has multiple stories and interpretations. The technique has a history, a reasoning, and it allows for creative thinking to explore further. With the javelin throw we can do the same. There are different philosophies of how to throw this thing, and it transcends many years now. While a specific position in the throw can be dissected to reveal the biomechanics of why we must do this to reach the highest potential for power, speed, and safety, the general principle remains the same for martial arts.

It is this dissection of an activity, the quest for the most relevant meaning which can be applied to any sport or physical hobby, that was developed so keenly during my time in the martial arts.

Hip action on Javelin throw

Author Information
William Pizii
WillPizii@gmail.com
https://sites.psu.edu/willpizii/

Will Pizii is a recent graduate of Penn State University and Schreyer's Honor College. He is a freelance writer and martial artist and is currently pursuing a career as a Copywriter and Copyeditor.

On the Record

By Vigiles Urbani

The Rules of Engagement in Self Defense

Liability—Direct and Vicarious

An introduction to the American legal systems (criminal/civil and state/federal) and types of liability (direct and vicarious)

3. What is the Threat? To answer this foundational question, it is important to understand a few core concepts. At least in the United States, there are two types of legal cases: **Criminal** and **Civil**. In the former, charges are brought by Police and Prosecutors. In the latter, cases are filed by private citizens, usually with the help of attorneys. There are also two separate legal systems: **State Court** and **Federal Court**. Criminal and civil cases may be brought in either system depending on a variety of factors, including location, identity of the parties, and nature of the **crime** or **tort** (civil wrong). Every state has a different set of statutes and a different body of **precedent** or **case-law**. Federal law—which may supersede or operate parallel with state law—is different again. Unfortunately, in the wake of a use-

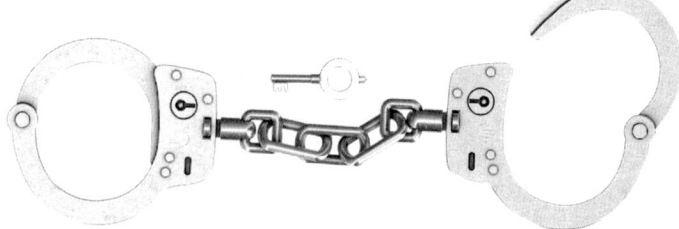

of-force incident, you can find yourself being dragged into any of these forums, and if you are an instructor, you don't even have to have been directly involved: Under certain circumstances, you can be held legally responsible not just for your own actions (**direct liability**), but also for those of another, like your student (**vicarious liability**). Do we have your attention now? Good!

> Case Study: Anderson v. Pressure Point Control Tactics, 145 P.3d 503 (Supreme Court of Alaska, 2006): In this case, Deborah Anderson, a corrections officer trainee, sustained a neck injury during use-of-force training provided by a private company ("PPCT"). Rather than suing the person who actually threw her (Michael Addington), Deborah instead sued the company that trained Addington under the theories of **vicarious liability** and *respondeat superior* **(master and servant).** And while Anderson did not ultimately prevail, it was not because these legal theories were dismissed; it was only because the facts of this specific case failed to show that PPCT exercised sufficient control over Addington. In other words, had the master-servant relationship been a little bit stronger, Anderson might well have prevailed. And either way, PPCT had to endure the time, expense, and embarrassment of years of litigation.

4. The Paralysis of Analysis: This is a lot to take in all at once. If you are feeling overwhelmed, don't despair. Unless you live in a high-risk region or do a dangerous job, trouble can be avoided most of the time. And in any event, if we don't want to live as hermits, we have no choice but to interact with the world around us. But if trouble comes looking for you, it helps to keep in mind the first rule of police work: Come home alive. You will—and should—do what it takes to survive. But by considering, and practicing,

various options *before* the need to employ them ever arises, you can front-load the analysis and avoid the need to make important decisions instantly and under highly stressful conditions, thereby increasing your chances of emerging from a confrontation without liability. Instructors: By making this a regular part of your classes, you can offer this same vital service to your students, thereby protecting them (and yourself) in the same way.

> Case Study: One of the toughest military operators on the planet teaches a brutal class on knife defense to advanced practitioners, at the end of which he poses the question: *"Do you know what I would do to a man who stuck a knife in my face and demanded my wallet?"* You can almost hear the students wondering, *"What would you do, what would you do, take his head off?"* This grizzled combat veteran then pauses, clears his throat, casts his eyes down, and answers: *"I would—give it to him. There is nothing in my wallet worth risking another scar, let alone my life..."*

TRADITIONAL MARTIAL ARTS INTERNATIONAL

Tanzenbukan Goju-Ryu

4th generation branch of Okinawan Goju-Ryu. Hanshi Marquez studied Goju-Ryu in Okinawa as a direct student of Masanobu Shijo (founder of Shobukan Goju-Ryu)

Kokusai Ryukyu Kobujutsu Kenkyokai

The comprehensive study of 3 classic weaponry systems organizing on the island of Okinawa. Jinbukan Kobudo, Rengokai Kobudo, Ufuchiku-Den Kobujutsu

TMAI Honbu – School of Hope

1000 Route 66 Ste H, Glendora, California
626-485-6716 ▪ www.tmai-honbu.com

Hanshi Anthony C. Marquez

Yin

By Donna Spiser

Women in the Martial Arts

How our Art was Saved by a Woman

The style of kung fu we practice has always had female practitioners. Our art, known today as "Won Hop Loong Chuan," originated in a Daoist temple in Central China. The Temple housed both monks and nuns who worked, learned, and practiced alongside each other. When the Temple was eventually destroyed during the Tang Dynasty, it was a female practitioner who saved the knowledge from the Temple and passed it down through her family line.

Great female warriors are not unheard of in China. In fact, stories of female warriors go back thousands of years. For example, the wife of King Wu Ding (ruled circa 1215 to 1190 B.C.) was Lady Hao (Fu Hao). Inscriptions in her tomb describe her as having been a military commander. She was supposed to have been a respected military leader with important generals serving under her. Also, thanks to Disney, everyone has heard of "Mulan." However, the story is based on a poem called The Ballad of Hua Mulan, which describes a heroic female warrior who took her father's place and served successfully for twelve years until she retired. The earliest accounts of Hua Mulan indicate she may have lived during the Northern Wei dynasty (circa 386 to 584 A.D.). In 617 A.D., Princess Pingyang helped her father, Li Yuan, defeat the forces of the Sui Dynasty and establish the Tang Dynasty. The Princess won the loyalty of other military leaders and eventually commanded an army of 70,000 men. She had a policy of not allowing her men to plunder, but instead to distribute food to peasants as they passed by. Her army, known as "The Army of the Lady," was welcomed by the people as liberators rather than invaders. Her assistance was so great in helping her father, Emperor Gaozu, that he honored her with a military funeral reserved for generals when she died in 623 A.D.

It was also not unheard of for men and women to live and be treated equally in Daoist monasteries in China. There are manuscripts dating from the early seventh century, such as the Fengdao Kenjie (Rules and Precepts for Worshiping the Dao), which outline proper behavior for monks and nuns and detail the way a Daoist monastery should function. In short, the only difference between men and women was the hat worn by females was larger than the hat worn by males. Otherwise, expectations for behavior, attire, and treatment were the same. The Fengdao Kejie was written prior to our Temple's destruction, so it reinforces our oral history that there were both male and female students.

Women and girls would have entered temples as nuns for many reasons. Poor families who dropped their daughters at temples may have wanted to save them from starvation or death due to diseases. Older girls entered temples to avoid an unwanted marriage or to have an opportunity to pursue an education. History also tells stories of widows, former concubines, and even princesses who became nuns. For women, just as men, a monastic life offered not only refuge and personal freedom, but also opportunities for an education that might not have been available outside the temple.

According to our oral tradition, men and women would have had the same daily routine. Basically, the schedule was to wake up, have a personal work out, wash, meditate, teach, wash, do group chores, eat a meal, and then study. Our Temple was based in Water Daoism, not Fire Daoism, so the routines and teachings were slightly different from other monasteries. Fire Daoism is more of a religion involving rituals, alchemy, and deities. Water Daoism is a way of viewing existence and understanding natural order. As Water Daoists, the focus was on personal development through meditation, studying, and working out. Part of the personal workouts included weapons training, forms, and other exercises for health. Consequently, the women in the Temple were trained just as men in weapons and fighting.

Our understanding is the Temple was destroyed during the latter part of the Tang Dynasty. Due to its strategic location and the politics of the time, the Temple stood in the way of a war lord with a large army. Prior to battle, women and children left the Temple and the invaders saw them as no threat. However, one of the greatest practitioners in the history of our art was a woman who had four sons with the head Abbot. She was a skilled warrior, and prior to the battle she left with one son walking beside her, one son being pushed in a cart, and she was pregnant with twins. Inside the cart, she was able to smuggle out the most important texts which had been produced at the Temple and preserve the knowledge of the monks.

Our heroine's story continued with her going on to have six more sons and several daughters. Additionally, she managed to exact revenge on the war lord responsible for the Temple's destruction. Posing as a concubine, she was able to enter his palace, assassinate him, and leave before anyone knew he was dead.

Although the Temple was physically destroyed, one woman was able to save the art from destruction. She passed down all the knowledge from the Temple to her children. The forms and teachings have continued to be passed down through subsequent generations of her family line. Sigung A.F. Walker is the adopted grandson of his teacher, Sensei Kushubi, who inherited everything through his family. While some katas have been added to the art over the centuries, nothing was lost thanks to one person being underestimated because she was a woman. As Lao Tzu teaches in The Tao Te Ching, "There is no greater catastrophe than underestimating the enemy." ☯

Author Information
Donna Spiser has practiced the Daoist art of Won Hop Loong Chuan and Wu Jia Tai Chi Chuan with Grandmaster A.F. Walker since the 1980's. She is ranked as a 4th degree blackbelt.
https://www.facebook.com/WonHop

Artwork: Brian Williams

Legends of the Ten Tigers

Tales of Martial Arts Masters

This book is a compilation of stories/tales of Martial Arts masters in the lineage of Won Hop Loong Chuan (Wan He Long Quan). These are tales that correspond to the history and dances found within the art.
by A. Flane Walker, Dr. Leslie Graham, 2020.

Dim Mak
Exposing the Mystery

A.F. Walker, J.B. Walters &
Leslie M. Graham, MS, DC, DAOM, LAc

Introduction

The goal of this column is to educate the reader on Dim Mak and its intricate Yin (陰) Yang (陽) relationship to both the martial and healing arts. In this edition of our Dim Mak column we will explore the health and martial usage of the acupuncture points Large Intestine-4 (LI-4, Hé Gǔ 合谷) and Liver-3 (LIV-3, Tài Chōng 太冲). We will describe the characteristics of these points, discuss the use of these acupuncture points in what modern Chinese medicine calls "the Four Gates" treatment, and then show how these same points can be used in a martial application.

Warning

The stimulation of LI-4 in pregnant women can induce labor, which could potentially cause a miscarriage. Do not, under any circumstances, stimulate LI-4 on a woman that is, or may be, pregnant.

This material set forth in this article is for informational or educational use only. Nothing contained in this article is, or should be considered, or used as a substitute for, medical advice, diagnosis, or treatment. Do not attempt to diagnose or treat medical conditions with the information provided within this article. Always seek medical treatment from licensed medical practitioners and acupuncture from Licensed and Certified Acupuncturists.

The applications shown in this article may cause lasting injury or even death. Do not, under any circumstances, strike someone on the acupuncture points or areas described within this article. This content is for informational purposes only.

The authors do not assume any responsibility for the use or misuse of information contained in this article.

Terminology

The term "Dim Mak" refers to the overall, ancient Chinese body of knowledge on the medical, health, and martial use of acupuncture points, herbalism, chi gung, massage, Tai Chi, weaponry, and hand patterns (kata). Today it is commonly thought of as a

specific type of strike which is said to kill the opponent. The study of Dim Mak entails a number of different types of attacks to acupuncture point combinations. These methods include:

Dim Ching Strike: A strike that will immediately incapacitate an opponent. This is usually caused due to a shock effect upon the central nervous system. A Dim Ching strike pattern may be modified to cause death, in which case it becomes a Dim Mak pattern.

Dim Hsueh Strike: A strike that targets what are known as "Blood Gates" within the body. A Blood Gate has an influence over the circulatory system of the body. Attacking a Blood Gate may incapacitate an opponent by causing a rapid drop in blood pressure. A Dim Hsueh strike pattern may be modified to cause death, in which case it becomes a Dim Mak pattern.

Dim Mak Strike: The nominal Dim Mak Strike is designed to kill an opponent after a period of time, usually three diurnal cycles (72 hours). The time period in which a particular strike combination is designed to manifest ranges from immediately to several years. Upon closer inspection of these strike combinations, we discover that they cause damage to internal organs that ultimately cause the death of the opponent.

In this article we demonstrate a Dim Hsueh strike.

Acupuncture Points

LI-4 "Joining Valleys"
合谷 Hé Gù

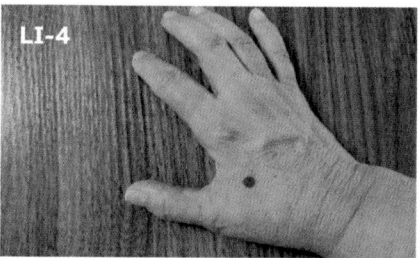

Chinese Medicine Characteristics

- Releases the exterior for wind-cold or wind-heat syndromes.
- Strengthens the *wei qi* (guardian qi), thereby improving immunity.
- Regulates the sweat glands, for excessive sweating.
- Any problem on the face—sense organs, mouth, teeth, jaw, toothache, allergies, rhinitis, hay fever, acne, eye problems, etc.
- Toothache use both LI-4 and ST-44—LI for the lower jaw and ST for the upper jaw.
- Headache, especially frontal and/or sinus (*Yangming* area).
- Chronic Pain.
- Influence the circulation of Qi and Blood—Use the four gates, LI-4 and LV-3 to move strongly the Qi and Blood in the body, clearing stagnation and alleviating pain.
- Promote labor or for the passing of a retained placenta.
- Emotional issues, dealing with grief or sadness

- *Ma Dan Yang* Heavenly Star Point for headache, fever and chills, or tooth decay. (Ma Dan Yang was one of the Seven Perfected Ones of the North, and during his lifetime composed an ode or song for these miraculous acupuncture points which were to be used for specific conditions. LI-4 was one of the original 11 points and then Liver-3 was added later after the passing of the Immortal Daoist Ma.)

Martial

- This is an extremely reactive point and should never be used on pregnant women. If used with SP-6, TW-5 (*San Jiao*) and PC-6, it can cause the fetus to abort.
- This is a setup point for a strike to LU-1 or LU-2. Done with a proper wrist hold, it can cause a lot of pain. Push in and up toward the elbow. A knock-out can be achieved by using the wrist hold and striking LU-5 down toward LU-7. The opponent's knees will buckle and his head will drop to his chest. This is usually a technique used in a wristlock.

Recovery

Cross the legs and put pressure on *Yin Tang*, rub deeply and put pressure on GB-20 in a counterclockwise circular motion. Also rub upward on the bilateral striking points.

LIV-3 "Great Surge (Rushing)" 太□_ Tài Chōng

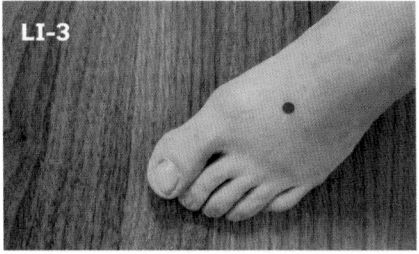

LI-3

Chinese Medicine Characteristics

- Generally, resolves stagnation and tonifies Yin—used for balancing liver pathologies.
- LV Qi Stagnation / LV Yang Rising—headaches, dizziness, canker sores.
- Eye issues—blurred vision, red, swollen, painful eyes.
- Menstrual issues from Deficient Blood, Yin, Qi and/or LV Qi Stagnation—dysmenorrhea, amenorrhea, PMS, breast tenderness.
- Genital issues—pain/swelling, hernia, impotence, seminal emission.
- Stagnation in the middle warmer—subcostal tension, chest/flank pain, swellings in the axillary region.
- Digestive issues from LV attacking ST/SP—nausea, vomiting, constipation, diarrhea with undigested food.

- Calming point—anger, irritability, insomnia, anxiety.
- With LI-4, four gates treatment—powerfully affects the flow of Qi and Blood throughout the body.
- Emotional issues, dealing with anger and irritability.
- Ma Dan Yang Heavenly Star Point for inability to walk, throat and breast issues, hernias, vision issues, sudden fits and convulsions.

Martial

- This is commonly used as a Dim Hsueh point. However, it is an extremely painful point.
- Coupled with a gallbladder strike (GB-24, GB-25, and, in particular, GB-15 or GB-14), it can achieve a knock-out. Usually when GB-24 or GB-25 is struck, vomiting may result. When struck hard, the recipient will grab the injured foot, drop to his back, and roll on the ground. Nausea is always present afterward.

Recovery

Lay the recipient of the strike on his back. Rub up the stomach meridian beginning at ST-41, paying particular attention to ST-38 and ST-34. Continue up the torso, rubbing GB-28 to GB-24 with deep intent. Nausea should stop quite quickly.

References
(1) Walker, A. F., & Bauer, R. (2014). *The Book of Dim Mak: Revised and updated.* Paladin Press. ISBN-10: 1610048784; ISBN-13: 978-1610048781

Health Application Treatment: The Four Gates

The Four Gates Treatment is a popular technique in acupuncture which helps to maintain the free flow of Qi and Blood throughout the body. It opens the meridians, increases circulation, reduces pain in the body, and serves to relax and calm the person. The treatment consists of stimulating LI-4 on each hand (Figure 3), and LV-3 on each foot (Figure 4). This may be accomplished by applying light finger pressure on one's own points, or upon those of another person.

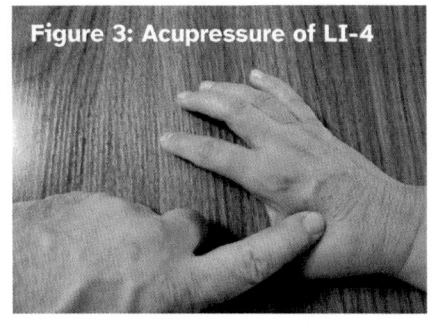

Figure 3: Acupressure of LI-4

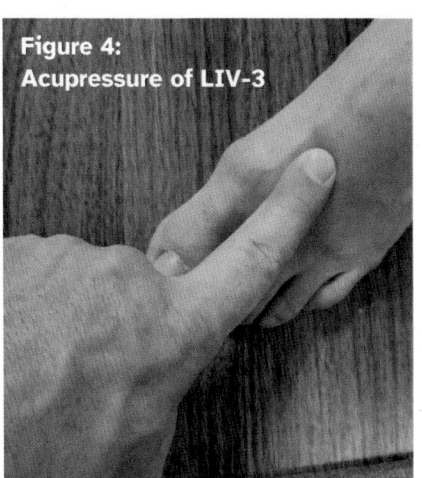

Figure 4: Acupressure of LIV-3

Martial Application

There is a general lack of knowledge regarding employment of acupuncture points in grappling situations within the larger martial arts community. Practitioners of various martial arts and sports do practice movements and leverages that apply pressure to acupuncture points without fully realizing how these points work and how they can be used more efficiently. Acupuncture points can be grasped and/or struck in a close grappling situation and may be used in defensive postures by smaller individuals, greatly enhancing the effectiveness of their techniques.

Many people consider the question, "How does one out-wrestle the grappler?" Attempting to do so places the defender in the position of being on the defensive and attempting to counter the opponent's strength and skills.

Instead, we look upon a grappling situation as one where the opponent has presented openings on his body and limited the actions of his arms and legs. We switch our mindset from one of defense to that of attacking. Our applications should always:

• Immediately place the attacker in a position where he can no longer attack us.

• Cause sufficient damage to the attacker such that he no longer poses a threat.

• Capitalize on their body's reactions to the points we are attacking.

• Be executed within one breath.

•Have no wasted movements.

• Be capable of placing the attacker's body on the ground according to the tactical situation. As an example, blocking the path of a second attacker to give us time to engage a third attacker.

Shifu Jay and Senpai Dan demonstrate a simple defense versus a rear bear hug (Figure 5). This defense utilizes striking Liver-3 and grasping Large Intestine-4. The defense illustrates the concept of immediately going on the offensive. The movement we are using to illustrate this technique is based upon

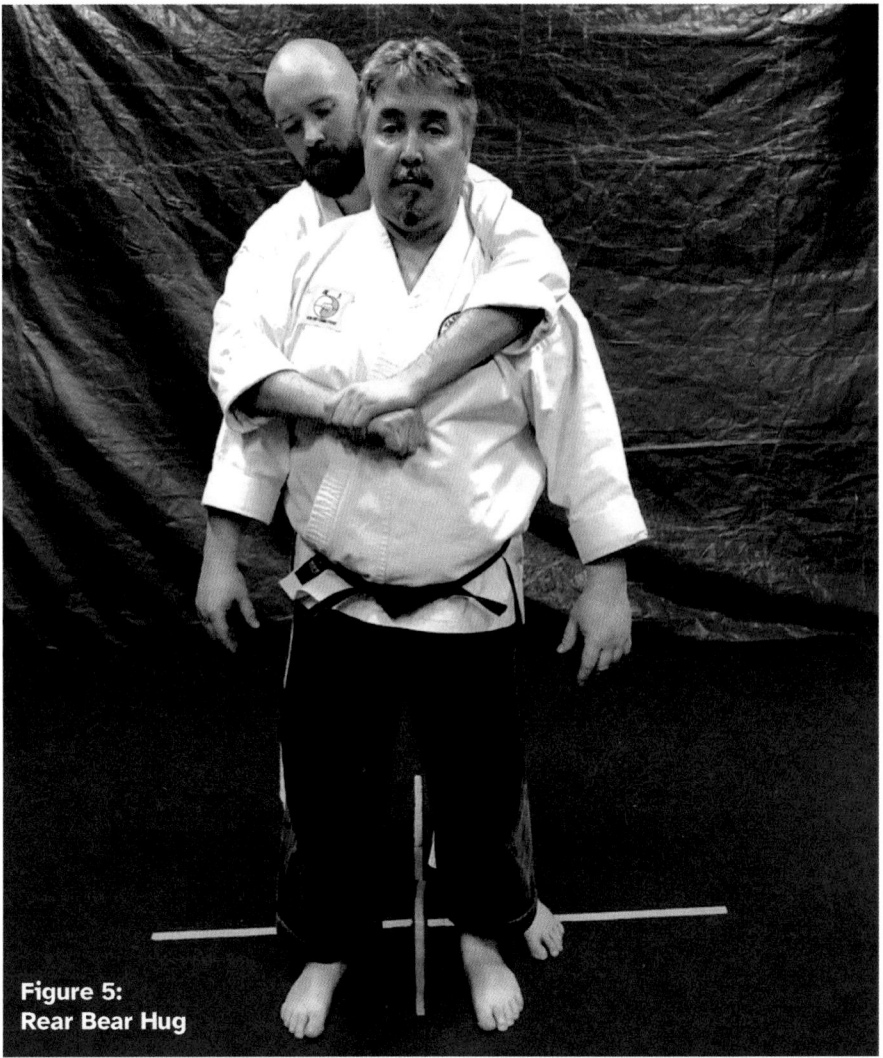

Figure 5:
Rear Bear Hug

Figure 6:
Grasp of LI-4

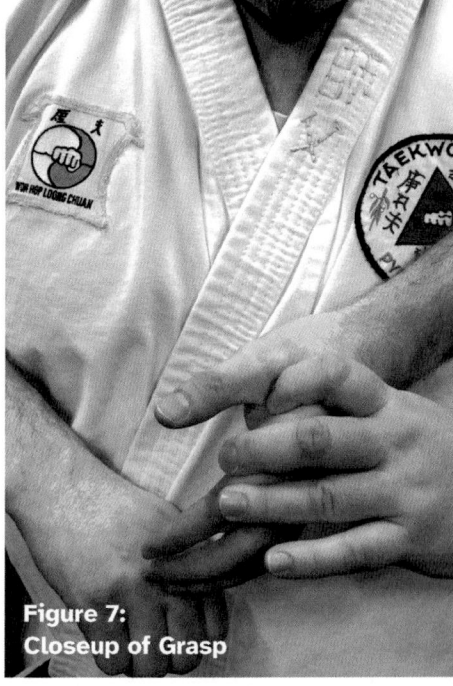

Figure 7:
Closeup of Grasp

Upon being grabbed Shifu Jay immediately grasps Senpai Dan's hand across the body (left to right hand, or right to left hand) such that he is pressing LI-4 (Figure 6 and 7).

Figure 8:
Foot Stomp

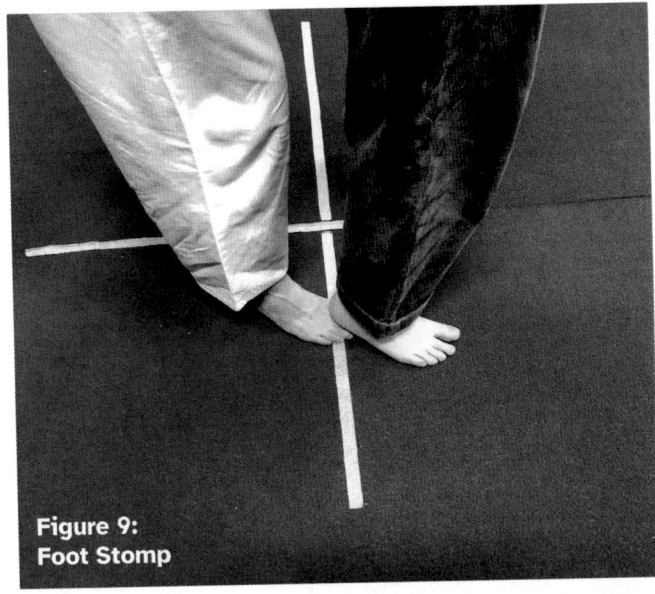

Figure 9:
Foot Stomp

Figure 10:
Thrown Setup

Figure 11:
Thrown Execution

the opening movement of the Okinawan dance Wanduan (King's Road).

Upon being grabbed Shifu Jay immediately grasps Senpai Dan's hand across the body (left to right hand, or right to left hand) such that he is pressing LI-4 (Figure 6 and 7).

Shifu Jay immediately stomps LIV-3 on the opposite side of the hand by which the attacker was grasped. The immediate effect of the stomp on LIV-3 is to take the strength out of the Senpai Dan's legs and to begin

dropping on the side of the stomp.

Shifu Jay then raises Senpai Dan's grasped hand, rotating it palm-up (Figure 10), and then executes a throw by rotating his arm to the side and down (Figure 11). The execution of the throw can be structured to either safely (for training) throw the attacker, or to damage the attacker's joints.

Summary

In this article we have shown how acupuncture points may be very beneficial from a health standpoint, and also be extremely useful in a fighting situation. We have extended the discussion of the use of acupuncture points and Dim Mak to include grabs, joint locks, and throws. The reader is invited to increase his or her knowledge of Dim Mak through the included references, or by contacting our organization for further discussions.

Author Information

James Walters at
james_b_walters@yahoo.com
https://www.karateatwo.org/

The Focused Warrior

By Victor Amat

Psychology and Combat Arts

"The past cannot be used to predict the future"

Nassim N. Taleb

The thinker and economist Nassim N. Taleb in his famous book, The Black Swan, warns us of what he calls a "fragile" society. The explanation of what he means, roughly, is simple: Human beings cannot predict with certainty the events that may happen. Today, for example, we are victims of a global pandemic that no state could prevent, despite the indicators that existed about our social fragility in case something like this broke out, and our responses are not sufficient to solve this challenge.

The practice of karate, and of martial arts in general, must provide training structures that make the person who practices someone with a greater capacity to adapt to the environment and to the tensions that may occur, both in real combat and in any situation of everyday life. Choki Motobu, in his writings, used to comment that karate should be "a school of life." And if this is so, we all know that difficulties in life lurk around every corner in unpredictable ways. One of the important mechanisms to generate self-confidence is assimilation of the fear of uncertainty in a way that our body responds efficiently and healthily. When we suffer from stress generated by unpredictable events, we endure a lot of muscular tension that prevents us from responding adequately to those stimuli. As a psychologist and coach, I have studied and reflected a lot on this topic.

Generally, in the traditional practice of karate, as in other combat arts, the training approaches are based on fixed schemes such as kata, or some forms

of bunkai. Also, the *kihon* (fundamentals) are organized predictably in most instances. Repetition work against a predetermined attack is an excellent way to generate automatisms that allow the practitioner's brain to respond unconsciously to these types of attacks, inhibiting the responses formed in the amygdala, the area of the brain that deals with fear management and survival. If we accept this hypothesis, the traditional practices of karate are excellent for training our neurology, making our body respond to an attack through constant repetition.

What would happen then, in a surprise attack or in response to a type of strike that we do not recognize?

Probably, our body cedes control to the amygdala and it responds through an attempt to escape, surrender in front of the opponent, or through defensive tension that could cause us to receive a good beating when resorting to crossing the arms over the head or adopting a fetal position.

Achieving an "anti-fragile" response requires a different approach. The first thing to take into account in training is what is necessary to perceive non-verbal indicators of aggressiveness in the environment, so that we can anticipate an attack? It would be the opposite of "*Karate ni sente nashi*" (there is no first attack in karate), if we do not take into account that this anticipation is a response to a real expression of hostility on the part of someone. Am I saying with this that we accept the risk of making mistakes and hitting who simply asked us for the time? Not at all, I'm saying that karate

practice should go beyond mere repetition of drills. Recognizing threats and assessing them properly also requires a certain amount of attention from the karateka.

A second option could be training with protective gear in which our partner can perform non-preset attacks, initially of minimal or moderate intensity, and thereby teach our body to respond. The practice of *Jissen* karate in the 1930s—Motobu's method of free-sparring with minimal rules or protective equipment—was an attempt to unify traditional practice with the need to apply techniques in scenarios of stress and in the face of unforeseeable circumstances.

It is no small matter if we want to give our karate an approach that is "anti-fragile" and allows us to gain self-confidence. Self-confidence requires perseverance and intelligent training, so practicing with different types of clothing, or in different scenarios would be a way to enrich our training, giving more credibility to the practice of martial arts.

The more we deepen the practice of techniques, the more we can realize their usefulness when we are able to perform them in the maximum range of possibilities and situations. Of course, it is very enriching to practice karate as aesthetic training, or simply as an entertaining form of calisthenics, but true lovers of the fighting arts are those who wish to strengthen their spirits in order to be valuable members of the community and thus be prepared for our own black swans. ☺

Author Information
Victor Amat
cetebreu@gmail.com
https://victoramat.es/

国際少林寺流唐手善徳会
International Shorinjiryu Tode Zentokukai

Kyan-Ha Karate

Oyakata Kobujitsu

Italy
Europe Director

Bruno Ballardini
Kyoshi, Nanadan 7°
Kigen Kan, Rome Italy

Zentokukai
Europe

Germany
Representative

Istvàn Tarnai
Seijitsu Kan
Neustadt, Germany

France
Representative

Anthony Pousset
Kyushin Kan
Valorbiquet, France

Italy
Representative

Michele Albiani
Nito no Tora Kan
Arezzo, Italy

Italy
Representative

David Poli
Kenshin Kan
Reggio Emilia, Italy

Italy
Representative

Francesco Ferrari
Kenshin Kan
Reggio Emilia, Italy

The Zentokukai has Dojos in the USA, Colombia, Italy, France and Germany
www.zentokukai.com

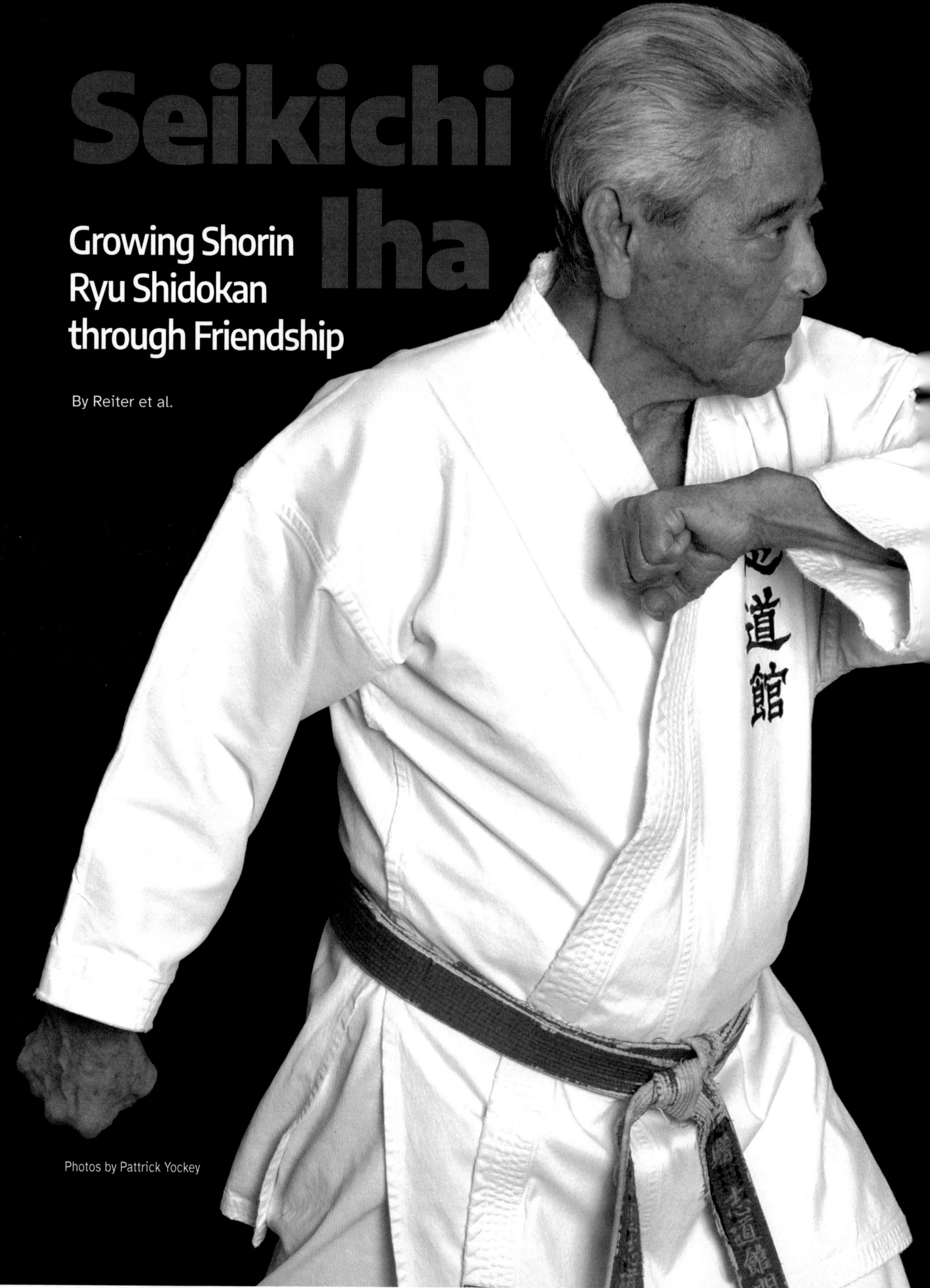

Seikichi Iha

Growing Shorin Ryu Shidokan through Friendship

By Reiter et al.

Photos by Pattrick Yockey

Seikichi Iha, Hanshi, 10th Dan, Shorin Ryu Shidokan, was born in 1932 in Tonabaru, Nishihara, Okinawa, JP. He studied under the noted Shuri-te lineage teachers, Shinpan Gusukuma and Katsuya Miyahira. Iha currently resides in Lansing, Michigan where he has taught at his Original Okinawa Karate dojo since 1975. As President of the Beikoku Shidokan Karatedo Association, he oversees instruction for a network of over 30 dojos. In 2020 Iha was the recipient of the Okinawa Prefecture Intangible Cultural Property Holder award for "extremely significant achievements in spreading Karate in Okinawa to the world for over 45 years." Seikichi Iha teaches self-defense through natural movement and believes that karate practice is beneficial for people of all ages. His longtime motto is "friendship, cooperation and learning."

Okinawa Hometown Beginnings

Seikichi Iha was born in 1932 in the village of Tonabaru, Nishihara, Okinawa, Japan (northeast of the historical Ryukuan capital of Shuri). When Iha was a child, resources were few but the close-knit community of family and friends provided a strong feeling of caring and tradition. Neighbors in the village were close and always looking out for each other. Iha fondly remembers as a child playing baseball in the street with only one base, using bats they made from sticks and balls from wound up string. (Later, he says baseball was curtailed because it was an American sport.) They also played a game of "touch head" that was kind of like wrestling.

Iha says that in those days there were no karate dojos. Karate was very specialized and teaching was done individually in private. No teachers earned a living from karate. Many old people talked about karate though and everyone had heard stories. There was respect shared when someone had a special celebration day and it was known that they studied karate. People in the village would note, "He did karate," with the greater emphasis on "did," the better they were.

WWII: Finding Hope in Hard Times

In 1945, the Battle of Okinawa changed everything. The devastating effects of the war would last for generations. Iha's village and the entire Nishihara area were completely destroyed along with most of Okinawa. It is estimated that 47% of the population in the entire Nishihara area ultimately lost their lives during the war.

Iha and his family and members of the village escaped to the south of Okinawa with many thousands of others seeking safety. He ended up in a civilian relocation camp on the Chinen peninsula for more than two years. Iha was in his early teens and remembers it as an extremely difficult time. Most people had lost family members and experienced great trauma. There was a dire shortage of food; many were injured or sick. Iha says, there was nothing to do to raise spirits—not even play music. Also

1970's Seikichi Iha training with makiwara at Original Okinawa Karate Dojo, Lansing MI.

living in the Chinen camp with Iha was Shuri-te master, Choshin Chibana. Chibana wanted to help give people hope, so he performed kata for them. Iha clearly remembers Chibana performing the kata Passai Dai. Young Iha was inspired by Choshin Chibana's demonstration of kata and his kindness during a time of great adversity.

Eventually, the families of Tonabaru were able to return home to rebuild, including families that had moved to mainland Japan to find work before the war. Iha says that after the war everyone was very upset and demoralized, so the village organized an event to help uplift the community with plays, storytelling, demonstrations, etc. Iha has vivid memories of Sabboro Maeshiro, who was a very small person, doing a dramatic demonstration of strength where he lay on the ground with a large rock on his stomach while someone broke the rock with a big hammer. Maeshiro, an Iha family friend, had lived in Osaka during the war and had picked up a few things like punching, street fighting techniques, and some Pinan kata. He could also do a double jump kick that could strike the ceiling with both feet at the same time. During 1948, Maeshiro introduced Iha to using a makiwara and got him more interested in learning karate.

Beginning Study with Shinpan Gusukuma

In 1950, Iha was introduced to his first formal karate teacher, Shinpan Gusukuma. Iha had a job working as a mechanic on an Army base, which was one of few places people could find a job then. At work, he became friends with a young man named Toshiro, who was a year older than Iha. Toshiro was the son of Shinpan Gusukuma's second wife. He took Iha to meet Gusukuma at his home in Gibo-cho, Shuri, and that visit was the beginning of Iha's formal karate training.

Shinpan Gusukuma, a student of Kanryo Higaonna and Anko Itosu, was very famous in Tonabara. He'd started a children's school in Nishihara before the war and many remembered him from that, including Iha's grandfather. He was known for his ability to help people in the community with injuries, using skills similar to those of a chiropractor or physical therapist today. There were also many stories about his athletic abilities such as high jumping like an Olympic gymnast. One story Iha tells describes how Gusukuma could run along the side of the rocky walls at Shuri-jo, similar to today's parkour. Iha says he was a small person and reportedly never changed in size from age 16.

People talked about how Gusukuma had lost his fingernails from practicing nukite techniques. Iha

小林流　宮平空手道場　'57.12.4

1957 Miyahira Dojo Class Photo. (Seikichi Iha, front row second from right; Shoei Miyazato, seated left of Katsuya Miyahira in front row: Seiko Iha, brother of Iha and photographer, back row in dark jacket)

notes that this was achieved by striking bundles of bamboo fibers, but other than missing fingernails, he says Gusukuma's hands were normal in appearance. (Iha also notes that Choshin Chibana and Katsuya Miyahira also had healthy-looking hands that were not disfigured from striking abuse.)

Gusukuma had a wide knowledge of Okinawan karate kata and many respected karate friends. According to Iha, before the war, Chotoku Kyan reportedly came every week to practice with Gusukuma. He also was close friends with Anbun Tokuda and Kenwa Mabuni before the war. Gusukuma studied both Naha and Shuri style karate but chose to focus on Shorin Ryu for its natural motion, quickness, and lack of tension. He was also dedicated to Zen practice and

could maintain focus for extended periods of time.

Iha rode the bus once or twice a week after work to Gusukuma's small, one-room house where he practiced

Shinpan Gusukuma

kata until he was exhausted and then received verbal corrections (homework) from his Sensei. Iha recalls the space being so small he would often have to back up to fit in a kata. Hopefully there would be time afterwards to have tea and Okinawan sugar and karate talk before he had to catch the last bus home. Some days when he got to the house Gusukuma wasn't there so Iha practiced his kata repeatedly and went home. In 1952, Gusukuma moved farther away to a two-room house in Naminoue, located on the west coast of Okinawa, north of Naha and next to the famous Naminoue-gu Shinto shrine. Training eventually moved inside the shrine where there was more space.

As a teacher, Iha says Gusukuma was very precise in his verbal instruction. His expectation was that the student practiced their homework repeatedly before more instruction would be given. Typical of teaching at that time, the teacher's words and methods were followed without question. Practice hard with full effort, demonstrate kata for Sensei, refine, repeat. Gusukuma told Iha that by practicing kata to the point of exhaustion you learn how to control your power. So, you can go from "0–100" in an instant, removing tension when you have to act and only using what power you needed. Gusukuma considered the personal study of bunkai (jutsu), oyo bunkai (ryaku) to be essential in order to understand the practical aspects of kata. Learning the habit of training with the spirit of endless refinement and practice carried Iha far through life's challenges.

Another important value that Gusukuma instilled in Iha was to keep a balance between work and karate. It was most important to have a job, then study karate in one's spare time. Also, never to use karate for the wrong reasons. (There was a lot of street fighting and bullying during the unsettled post-war years.)

Abruptly, in 1954, after a 3-day illness, Shinpan Gusukuma passed away in his sleep.

Katsuya Miyahira and Shidokan Dojo

Left without a teacher, Iha's neighbor in Tonabaru, Shoei Miyazato, introduced Iha to his teacher from the same Shuri-te lineage, Katsuya Miyahira, who had a dojo in Naha. Iha came to the dojo, bringing other students from Gusukuma's dojo. Later, in 1956, Miyahira built the Shidokan dojo behind his house at Tsuboya, Naha, and moved classes there.

Katsuya Miyahira was a student of Choshin Chibana, Anbun Tokuda and Choki Motobu. His belief in teaching karate was to help make people strong so they could survive adversity. He had observed first-hand during his years teaching in Manchuria how people who couldn't defend themselves were the first to die in conflict and felt the study of karate could help prevent this. Iha also

Shinpan Gusukuma, back row, upper left; Choshin Chibana, back row 3rd from left

points out that in Okinawa after World War II it was important to know how to protect oneself. Iha says of Miyahira Sensei that he was very well-respected in the community and kind. He treated Iha like family.

During the Miyahira dojo classes, the focus was on kata practice and correction. Iha was assigned to work with the beginning students and he and Shoei Miyazato also helped recruit more students. After classes, they would often continue to train together at the dojo and back at home in Tanabaru, working on partnership, bunkai, and oyo bunkai. This time together built what would become a lifelong friendship spanning years and

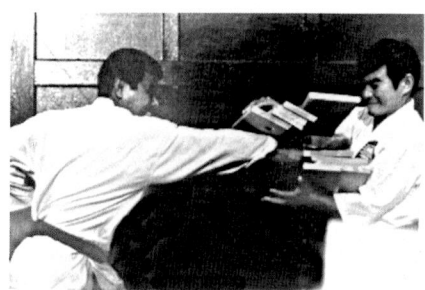

Seikichi Iha (left), Seigi Shiroma (right)

1957 karate training at old Miyahira dojo courtyard in Naha, Okinawa. (*Photo by Seiko Iha.*)

continents.

While training at the Miyahira dojo, Iha was asked by his Sensei to perform karate at special events such as representing Shorin Ryu at a sports event on the Japanese mainland (1955); for guests at a Japanese boxing tournament in Naha (1963); and group demonstrations of karate for a Tokyo television show (1964).

In 1964, Iha was selected to perform a kata at the 50th

Seikichi Iha and Shoei Miyazato kumite training and Seikichi Iha kata training in their home town of Tonabaru, Nishihara. Shoei Miyazato introduced Iha to the Miyahira dojo after the passing of Shinpan Gusukuma. They remained lifelong friends. (*Photos by Seiko Iha.*)

anniversary unveiling ceremony of the monument to Anko Itosu erected by Chosin Chibana in memory of Anko Itosu's death. He performed the kata Passai Sho (Itosu Passai).

Iha says that in his younger years he often enjoyed performing the Kusanku kata for solo demonstrations. In recent years his preference has been to perform Gojushiho. When frequently asked by students if he has a "favorite" kata, he will often say "all of them" and notes that one's least liked kata are the ones to work on. They will likely become your new favorites after focused study and practice.

Expanding Experiences
The late 1960s were a time of growth and exploration. In 1965, Iha was sent by Miyahira to work for 11 months as an advisor at the dojo of Latino Gonzales in Manilla, Philippines. Returning home, he trained Marines on the Futenma base and also started a dojo in his home town. There wasn't much opportunity at that time in

Unveiling ceremony for the monument of Anko Itosu, erected by Choshin Chibana, beside the Itosu gravesite in the forest of Furushima in Mawashi on August 30, 1964 to commemorate the 50th anniversary of the master's death. Four students (Iko Oshiro, a student of Higa; Katsuyuki Shimabukuro, a student of Chibana; Takeshi Miyagi, a student of Miyahira; Seikichi Iha, a student of Miyahira) were selected to perform a kata demonstration in Itosu's memory.

1964 karate demonstration group in Tokyo, Japan. (Left to right, front row: Kazo Mori, Seiko Fukuchi (Goju-ryu), Seikichi Iha (Shorin-ryu) Back row: Chokei Kishaba and Kensai Taba (Matsubayashi-ryu).) Iha says this group made up of members from various Okinawan ryu was selected to do karate demonstrations and interviews in various Tokyo locations including on television.

KARATE

SHIDO-KAN DOJO
5403 WEST PICO BLVD.
LOS ANGELES, CALIF. 90019

Seikichi Iha, 1970 Shidokan Dojo Brochure, Los Angeles, CA

Okinawa but the interest in karate in the Unites States was growing rapidly, especially in the area around Hollywood. In 1967, Iha visited Los Angeles, California, with friends and visited several dojos, meeting Hollywood celebrities like Ed Parker, Chuck Norris, and Bruce Lee.

Iha taught karate for five months at the Okinawan Club in Los Angeles, then opened the Shureikan dojo. He appeared on TV; Black Belt magazine ran a feature interview with Seikichi Iha, Kensai Taba and Seijun Kina in 1968; Karate Illustrated did a photo spread of Iha performing kata in 1970. In 1969, Iha traveled to Guam to help his friend Seigi Shiroma open a dojo there and then came back to Los Angeles to open the Shidokan dojo.

While teaching in Los Angeles, Iha observed that students tended to focus on being strong and competing with each other. Iha felt that a better way to become stronger was to make friends who, through partnership work, could help each other improve.

Bringing Shidokan to Michigan

The karate scene in Los Angeles was quickly becoming oversaturated so, in 1974, on the invitation of students of Tadashi Yamashita who he'd met in Los Angeles in 1970, Iha visited Lansing, Michigan, with his friend Toshiyuki Itokazu (Uechi Ryu). Iha has resided in Lansing ever since, teaching at his "Original Okinawa Karate" dojo located between Michigan State University and the Michigan State Capitol.

There was plenty of work to do to build a traditional Okinawan karate dojo in Lansing, with no funds and a little English. Iha says this is where the habits of hard practice and taking personal responsibility from his early training days in Okinawa were so important. The times with Gusukuma when he was challenged to perform kata in front of his teacher, nervous and shaking to the point of exhaustion, or being charged by his teacher with endlessly hitting the makiwara to try and achieve power three times his weight—these were some of the lessons in perseverance

1963 Miyahira dojo demonstration for guests of Japan boxing tournament, Naha, Okinawa. Seikichi Iha performing tile breaking. (Photos, Seiko Iha)

he credits with helping carry him forward in growing a new dojo and community. He knew he had to train hard at home, work a physically demanding day job to make ends meet, and show up every day at the dojo giving students his best effort no matter how tired he might be.

Iha says he wanted to make karate accessible to everyone—women, men, children, people of all ages and

Seikichi Iha performing performing kata at 1963 Miyahira dojo demisntration. (Photos, Seiko Iha)

Karatedo Association, Iha began training events to bring the Beikoku Shidokan dojos together—also inviting members of the international Shidokan community and other ryu-ha—to share training ideas and build more friendships. In 1996, Katsuya Miyahira, came to East Lansing for the 20th Anniversary celebration of Beikoku Shidokan.

On March 25, 2001, Iha was promoted to Hanshi, 10th Dan, by his teacher, Miyahira Katsuya. Iha has traveled frequently with his students, teaching seminars and promoting exchange of international friendship. Iha has mentioned the Okinawan idea of ichariba chode (roughly translated as, "once we have met we are friends for life") and it is evident in the feelings of friendship created during his seminars.

Honoring Karate's Okinawan Heritage

Helping his students grow an awareness and appreciation of karate's roots in Okinawan history and culture has been important for Iha. Over the years he has taken many students to Okinawa to visit historical sites and experience karate there. He is a member of the Michigan Okinawa

physical abilities—and make the dojo a place that built friendships through training. He realized that some of the traditional teaching methods used in Okinawa, such as repetitive kata practice with never questioning the teacher, were not going to work as well in the U.S. culture. American students expected to be able to ask lots of questions of their teachers and tired easily of repetitive training, requiring a variety of activities during the dojo classes to keep training interesting. This took a lot of work, creativity, and patience.

With the help of friends and tireless effort, Iha was able to recruit students who were excited to learn. Classes included a curriculum of kata, partner drills, and kumite. Iha also developed bunkai and oyo bunkai for groups of four to five people to help build teamwork.

Iha's driving philosophy, "Friendship, Cooperation, Learning" has been the key to his success in keeping students engaged in learning for decades. Karate "body language" becomes a "conversation" through partnership. Partnership makes friendship better. With cooperation (not competition), both win and nobody loses.

Branching Out

Over the years, as Iha's students began to move on to jobs in other cities, states, and countries, they formed new dojos and came back to Lansing with their students for more instruction. In the 1990s under the umbrella of the Beikoku Shidokan

Katsuya Miyahira giving a presentation on karate history to members during the 1996 National Training Seminar (NTS) and 20th anniversary celebration of the Beikoku Shidokan Karatedo Association at Michigan State University, East Lansing, Michigan. (Photo by Pattrick Yockey.)

Kenjin Kai, encouraging his students to attend and perform demonstrations at cultural events. He often talks about his deep appreciation to the Okinawa Club members in Los Angeles who helped him get started in the U.S. In 2008, the State of Michigan Governor's Awards for Arts and Culture presented Seikichi Iha with the Michigan Heritage Award for "passing on of Okinawan marital arts with excellence and authenticity."

In August 2019, over 300 members of the Beikoku Shidokan Association gathered in Naha, Okinawa, in honor of Iha's Tookachi (88th Birthday) celebration which included a weekend of friendship seminars and demonstrations of karate and kobudo at the Okinawa Karate Kaikan. Attendees visited historical karate and cultural sites and spent an emotionally moving day at the Peace Park.

Karate in the Time of COVID-19

In March 2020, along with dojos everywhere, the Original Okinawa Karate dojo in Lansing closed for in-person training due to COVID-19. Iha has been patiently waiting at his home in Lansing since that time. This hasn't stopped him from staying busy at home—gardening vegetables and enjoying nature, practicing Sanshin, working on his karate daily, staying connected with students by phone and Zoom, and teaching instructors remotely. Always optimistic, he's learning what he can do with new tools. He cheers up his students with "Ganbarimashou!" ("Keep doing!") on Zoom meetings.

On May 19, 2020, Seikichi Iha received a call from the Okinawa Prefecture that he had been selected as one of the six 2020 recipients of the Okinawa Prefecture Intangible Cultural Property Holder award for Karate and Kobudo. The stated purpose of this award is "to continue to preserve and pass on the traditional culture of Okinawa that has

April 2020, Seikichi Iha encourages Beikoku Shidokan Instructors from his home in Lansing, Michigan via Zoom during 2020 pandemic shutdown. (Photo by Fortunato Restagno.)

been preserved and passed down through generations." He was recognized for his "extremely significant achievements in spreading Karate in Okinawa to the world for over 45 years." Although due to the pandemic, he was not able to travel to Okinawa for the ceremonies, he hopes to be able to celebrate on the next Karate Day in Okinawa in October 2021.

In July 2020, due to COVID-19, the annual Beikoku Shidokan training seminar was held via Zoom. Hundreds of participants joined in from all over the world to watch Iha teaching from the backyard of his house.

2019 Seikichi Iha, Tookachi Friendship Seminar, Okinawa Karate Kaikan (Photo by Pattrick Yockey.)

Karate for Life

Iha frequently says that the greatest benefit of karate for him has been all the friendships, going back to the early years of training with his neighborhood friend, Shoei Miyazato. He says with karate friendships, 10–20 years can pass without seeing each other in person, but the connections of friendship and karate continue to be strong.

When asked what advice he can give to help others from his perspective as a life-long student of karate, Iha says,

you have to figure it out for yourself because everybody is different. Practice until you are tired—karate motion will make you stronger. Find a good partner you enjoy practicing with and practice often. Make friends, make training fun, and you will be happy!

In closing, Seikichi Iha says that the COVID-19 pandemic has made him even more appreciative of people coming together to take care of others during difficult times. He

wishes to share his sincere gratitude for the support of his family, friends, students, and the global community throughout his life-long karate journey. ○

Author Information

History and photos provided by Seikichi Iha, Hanshi, 10th Dan, Shorin-Ryu Shidokan. (Assisting students: Marian Reiter, 6th Dan, writer, interviewer; Mark McCloud, 8th Dan, interviewer and reviewer; Matthew Hubinger, 7th Dan, interviewer and reviewer)

August 2019, Seikichi Iha and Beikoku Shidokan attendees at Shuri-jo. (Photo by Pattrick Yockey)

Foundations of Movement

At the core of Iha's teaching has been the idea of natural motion, free of tension or excess movement. His compilation of The Essential Teachings of Shidokan Karate-do encapsulates for his students the Shidokan Shorin Ryu principles of the teachers who influenced him.

Choshin Chibana: Don't show (off) your abilities or intention. Be modest in behavior (kenkyo) and natural in movement (shizentai).

Meaning: True karateka do not announce themselves, but remain in a modest state of continual and natural readiness that is neither exhausting through tension nor apparent to others. Through proper body control (sabaki: balance, breathing, muscle tension, facial expression), their karate is only seen or felt at the critical moment. This has the double-meaning of neither showing off in a proud manner nor making unnecessary movements in actual applications. Iha Sensei said the idea of "not showing what you know" is like a person holding two, one-gallon jars—one empty, one full and heavy—with the difference between their weights not revealed by how they are held. Similarly, karate should ideally be unobservable until the moment it is necessary to use. "The capable hawk hides its talons."

Shinpan Gusukuma: No 'over-motion' (wabadi), only natural (shizen) motion.

Meaning: Excessive movement (wabadi, "over motion") will not work in application. It will be too late and is easily overcome. Natural movement is always "just enough," like catching or throwing a ball. Realize, too, that shizentai (natural body position, as at the start of kata) is a stance of patience. It is the perfect outward expression of an inward disposition for a martial artist, and for a human being. Injuries, misunderstandings, personal obligations, and long periods of stagnation are critical to our development. Each

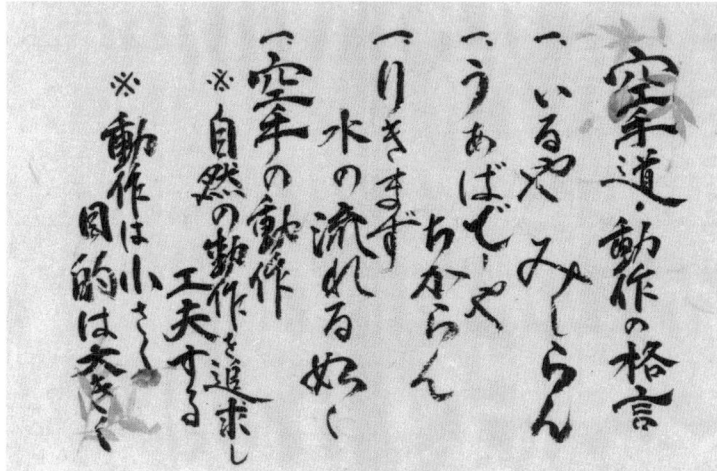

The Essentials of Shidokan Teaching

struggle refines our character into that of a martial artist to produce martial virtue (butoku). Accept difficulties as normal stepping-stones in your training. Be patient in your practice. "Having patience where patience is intolerable, this is true patience."

Katsuya Miyahira: Natural movement has no straining tension. "Flowing water competes with nothing." (Ryusui saki wo kisuwazu.)

Meaning: Movement is relaxed and focused only at the end. This lets power flow out of the body like water from a hose or water in a stream. It doesn't fight against itself or others. Excessive tension in the muscles and tendons traps power in the body. Moreover, just as water doesn't fight against the rocks in the river, so too the receiving of an attack is done with flowing and enveloping energy, not clashing. This is at the heart of nagashi waza, flowing techniques.

Seikichi Iha: Proper partner work leads to natural movement which, while small and unseen, yields great

Choshin Chibana

Katsuya Miyahira

opportunities for your martial purposes. This creates the quality of elegance in movement.

Meaning: All effective techniques seem hidden because they are so natural as to appear nonchalant or accidental. There is no thought attached to them (mushin). But this refined elegance only comes from proper partner work which is based upon cooperation and care for each other, and not through a competitive spirit where there can only be one winner and one loser. A competitive mind undermines growth because it is based upon ego satisfaction, which clouds self-perception. Growth only comes from seeing one's self in an honest way, which our partners can show to us if we listen with our minds and bodies (which Iha Sensei here calls "body conversation"). Mushin (an unattached mind) is the proper mental state of executing movement at the critical moment and humility is the proper mental state for learning movement. Sensei often reminds us to "make friends with karate." Our heart techniques (kokoro waza) most fully develop from martial friendship (buyu). ☺

1988 Katsuya Miyahira and Seikichi Iha at the Shidokan Dojo, Naha, Okinawa

"The Essential Teachings of Shidokan Karatedo" are provided by Seikichi Iha, assisted by Akiyoshi Shiroma with Japanese calligraphy by Nobuo Shimabukuro. English translations of Japanese text by Seikichi Iha assisted by Yujiro Uza. Meaning of concepts compiled from interviews with Seikichi Iha by Matthew Hubinger, Marian Reiter and Mark McCloud, May 2016.

THE FUTURE OF TRADITIONAL BUDO

By Franco Sanguinetti

What can we expect from the future Budoka in one or two generations?

The Old Days
Living in South America, January 1972 marked the initiation of my journey in the traditional martial arts: Japanese/Okinawan karate and kobudo. Like most martial artists in those days, when I started my path I never set a specific goal either to what belt I wanted to reach nor how long I was planning to continue training. I was just genuinely excited to be able to find the right fit for my introduction to the Arts. For many years I was looking for a dojo where I was going to be able to learn not only the technical and physical aspects of the traditional martial arts, but also the philosophical ones as well.

Not too long after I started my training, the martial arts in the Western world started to gain popularity following some benchmarks such as the TV series Kung Fu starring David Carradine in 1972, the launching of the movie Enter the Dragon starring Bruce Lee in 1973, and later on in 1984 The Karate Kid starring Pat Morita as the famous Mr. Miyagi.
Needless to say, all those film productions and some other ones

helped to promote the martial arts throughout the Western world. I remember clearly as a young practitioner attending a particular movie theater in a far and sketchy part of town where often during their Sunday 7:00 p.m. movie slot they would show martial arts movies. With some of them you would be able to take something away to help you with your training but some other ones would just be flashy with non-realistic content.

What was important to notice was that by the time the movie was over and the theater would turn the lights on, you would realize that the cinema audience was in its majority formed by young martial artists like myself. Many of us traveling from far away to that sketchy and dangerous part of town would show up at the theater "packing" nunchaku (a martial arts weapon consisting of two short sticks connected with a rope or chain)

hidden in our back just in case the situation might require "a little help from our friends" because it was obvious that we didn't belong in that part of town.

During those days we did not have the luxury to learn, sitting in the comfort of our home, from "YouTube Sensei" or by "Googling" for martial arts movies or literature. Being in South America, finding books or martial arts literature written in English was almost nonexistent, and in Spanish or translated to Spanish was something unheard of.

We practitioners were hungry to learn so we were willing to go out of our way to do what was necessary to keep learning. But it is also important to note that we practitioners were raised under an old school mentality, conditioned to respect for a higher authority, accountable for our actions, and really putting our best in whatever endeavor we pursued were the normal rules that we followed.

As part of that old school mentality that we grew up with, on a regular basis we would go through tough and severe training conditions without any hesitation or complaints just because we could see the important benefits to be gained. I remember clearly when I moved to live in Okinawa in 1982 in the middle of July when the heat and humidity are extremely high every day; on top of the severe

training that we endured in every class, we would need to survive the weather inside the dojo, too. Our dojo was not only small, but our sensei would close the only door to the outside of the structure, and the only window was a 24 by 12-inch opening inside the only bathroom at the dojo—and that window was always closed anyway. Whoever has trained martial arts in Okinawa in the middle of July can understand that concept.

Just considering the martial arts students from my own generation, it is remarkably easy to see the difference when comparing them to current practitioners. Nowadays, when I mention to the average practitioner that when I started my journey in budo (martial ways) I would train every day, Monday to Saturday at my dojo and Sunday at my house because my dojo was closed, they look at me as if I were an alien from another planet. When, on top of that, I share that my training days at the dojo every day included a two-hour class followed by two hours of jibun de renshu (my own training), they do not know anymore where even to begin to categorize me.

From the beginning of my training in the path of budo, I always considered that classes were for the students to receive instruction but in order to progress we would need to take that instruction to the next level; not to wait for the next class to see if we remembered what we had been

In the early 1980s when I lived in Okinawa, still in the "old school days," Higaonna Morio Sensei liked to use me as his *uke* (training partner) to demonstrate *shime* (testing) during Sanchin (breathing form) kata, especially when we had visitors at the dojo. I remember clearly one particular occasion when a group of instructors from Tokyo in mainland Japan arrived at our dojo, Higaonna Sensei asked me to demonstrate shime once again. Since I would do shime with him on a regular basis I was ready to do it again, but on that particular occasion between our morning and evening training sessions, I had developed severe sunburn on my shoulders and back. I had to use my "old school" upbringing to overcome the unpleasant feeling of being tested (slapped) on very tender, sunburned skin. Nowadays in many dojo, shime is considered "adult abuse".

taught, but more importantly to train on our own to honor that instruction by showing our sensei (person born before/commonly translated in the Western world as instructor) that we were putting in extra effort to develop a better waza (technique).

Considering the way that I grew up following the "old school" methods, after my humble 49 years in my journey training, teaching, and promoting the traditional martial arts of karate and kobudo, I can say that a good number of my doshi (fellow practitioners) that started their practice around the same time that I did, are today still active in their training. Evidently, through the number of years we all have evolved

in different directions; some continued in the Arts as practitioners, fewer continued training and teaching, and even fewer dedicated to train, teach, and promote. But in all, a nice group of my contemporary doshi is still active.

Identifying a Reality
From the inception of our humble dojo in San Diego, California, in 1985, I have never been motivated to start our training facilities thinking of generating money—my main focus and purpose always has been to pass the traditional arts of karate and kobudo to our students as I received them, and hopefully with time to contribute to those Arts by passing

them on to the next generations unchanged.

As part of that true and honest desire to provide our students with more classes without considering asking for additional fees, we initiated our dojo offering unlimited classes to all our students. Soon we were able to see our "gung-ho" students coming to classes five to six days per week; we would see them participating in as many karate and kobudo classes as possible at the beginning.

Unfortunately, with time we learned that even our group of "gung-ho" super dedicated students soon or later would get "burned out" from being at the dojo five to six days per week. As part of my nature to be honest with myself, I started to question my abilities as an instructor to figure out if I was failing to keep our students engaged in their training. Furthermore, due to my availability to travel to teach seminars and gasshuku (commonly translated in the western world as camps) throughout the USA and the many countries around the world where we have affiliated dojo, I started to make inquiries to other instructors regarding their similar experiences and trying to reach the roots of the problem.

Realization

After several years of honest research comparing experiences and teaching methods with other instructors in the USA and around the world, I came for the first time to the sad conclusion

Five-year-old, serious practitioner from the Day Care Center Program learning how to block a two-handed attack with focus shield.

that the problem of students dropping their training was not in any way related to my teaching methods or the number of classes that I provided to them; it was the simply the fact society was no longer the same as when I was a kid or as when I was younger growing up in the martial arts.

This sad realization wasn't a reality or a phenomenon found only in the USA, this was a reality that I was able to personally experience and see with my own eyes in the five different continents around the world where I have had the opportunity to travel and teach. The most remarkable, and perhaps most personal disappointment in the matter, is that in my personal journey researching

this new reality I was able to see and realize with my own eyes that the phenomenon had already reached the roots of our Arts, in the children on Okinawa, the birthplace of karate and kobudo.

Through my personal, yearly trips to train in Okinawa and also my yearly trips of taking our students to train on this special Island, I have been able to hear from Okinawan instructors how sad they are with the reality that Okinawan children are more interested in sports such as soccer, baseball, and even golf, over karate and kobudo.

Not that I needed extra confirmation, but in addition to my findings, for a period of five years we had next to our dojo one of those

Sanguinetti Sensei practicing *Seiyunchin* with part of the adult and teenage members of the Bushikan Mentor Program, outside his dojo due to COVID-19 restrictions.

CrossFit gyms that at one point were very popular and fashionable across the USA. During the five years that their business lasted we were able to see that as fast as new customers signed up at the gym, almost equally quickly they quit. All these new, motivated, and ready to work-out customers would arrive at the facility with the purest intentions to get fit, but as soon as they realized that in order to look as toned as the gym instructors they would need to discipline themselves not only in having consistent, methodic, physical training, but also they would need to discipline themselves in their eating habits, the result was they quit when seeing how much work was involved.

Needless to say, these were primarily young adults that already had grown up and were molded by the new set of norms and social influences that we will describe later on. The gym instructors were very eager to train all those new customers but the patrons, even though they were interested to go through the program, weren't equipped to do so. Sad to say, at the end of those five years we at the dojo weren't able to count even on one hand the members of the gym that stayed and trained the whole period of that time.

How Did We Get to This Point?

As a natural evolution from the elements of my generation growing up with parents that were very strict with us, parents that would not only have high expectations of us but equally importantly, accountability for our actions, now as adults and in many cases now as parents of young kids my generation has opted to change the way that they were raised to adopt a newer method to educate their children. As part of that new approach with their own kids they often opt to say to me "my parents were very tough on me so now that I am a parent, I want to treat my child differently, I want to be my child's friend." Many of these new parents recollect their disciplinary days and try to be better parents than their own, and have now done a 180-degree turn trying to be more "philosophic" with their children.

So, as part of their new effort to educate their own children differently, trying to be nice to them and avoid any discipline that reminds them of their own childhoods, many of them have let their kids pretty much do at home whatever they want and as a result, become the ones that run those households. As expected, the great majority of those children are growing up with no boundaries, no expectations, no accountability, no discipline, and not knowing how to work hard for something. In addition

Sanguinetti Sensei "planting as many young, five-gallon trees" as possible at one of the elementary schools in his district through one of the School Programs. Young students practicing basic techniques.

Sanguinetti Sensei applying one of the core concepts of his successful Mentor Program: As part of his traditional procedure at his dojo to emphasize the importance of honoring every single rank earned, he is putting a new black-belt on one of his teenagers.

to this new trend of education, cellular phones, tablets, and personal computers that were only a part of science fiction movies when I was a kid, as well as the phenomenon of social media that has overloaded the world for at least the last decade, have played an important role influencing our kids and young adults. Most noticeable are the effects of the sentiment of entitlement, the desire for quick gratification, short spans of attention, a lack of the ability to resolve problems, etc.

Also, many of our newer parents are trying to provide their children with things or activities that they were not able to have or participate in when they were kids, such as music, sports, and/or in general special undertakings, and are now many times overloading their own children with too many activities. Nowadays it is very common to see kids that will have an organized schedule every day, trying to participate in four or five different disciplines, sports, or activities each week. In some more extreme cases you also will see children jumping in the same day from activity to activity, many times changing uniforms or clothing inside their parent's cars as they are being driven from one place to the other.

If all these different factors were not enough to affect the way our children are growing up nowadays, a significant difference from when I was a child is the fact divorce has become a normal social circumstance in society, being more predominant in some areas than others. More children than we would like to see are growing up having two separate homes, many times two different sets of values and guidance, which in all affects them in many aspects of their lives such as focus, concentration, and insecurity, among many others.

So How is All This New Social Phenomena Reflected in a Dojo?
It is refreshing to know that even considering the world that kids are growing up in nowadays, you are still able to find children whose parents have instilled in them old values, so that by the time they show up in a traditional dojo they not only can adapt to it, but also flourish in it. Unfortunately, considering all the common factors that we have described above, it is more common that a large majority of children showing up in a traditional dojo are going to have a culture shock. Those will be the kids who more than likely when joining a regular class will be complaining during the session "the class is too hard," "the class is too

long," "I'm tired," "I'm thirsty," etc.

The culture shock they find in a traditional dojo, where they are being pushed to perform faster, harder, and better, to be accountable for their action, to help others, etc., usually translates to kids telling their parents that they do not like the martial arts.

McDojos: An Additional Problem
In all industries we can find those who want to do what is right, thinking of creating not only something that will last for a long time but also something that will bring new customers in the future due to their ethics and good practices. But on the other hand, there are those who do not care to strive for excellence, but rather prefer to cut corners, thinking just of making money at the moment. Well, the martial arts industry is no different. We have always had good, conscientious, and dedicated traditional instructors that will go out of their way to spread the Arts the correct way, forming a solid group of students that are the future of their dojo and the future of traditional budo. That kind of dojo will keep a hard and disciplined curriculum to produce not only physically but also mentally and emotionally tough students who understand and preserve the nature and integrity of

Five-year-old little Nicolla receiving her 9th Kyu in karate from her Dad, Sanguinetti Sensei. She is one of the dojo students that has benefited from the "old school" mentality taught at his dojo. "I have been practicing martial arts since I was three years old. The philosophy of traditional martial arts was and is an ever-present aspect of my life both on and off the floor. Martial arts are simply a part of who I am, for which I will always be grateful. The benefits are not just in what it teaches your body, but in what it teaches your mind and your soul."

commercially claiming to have 300 or more students as a sign of success. In order to not only obtain that high a number of students but also to retain them, this type of school will apply typical commercial practices such as short and easy classes, all kind of belts, patches, and gimmicks, and of course the offer for a black-belt in the short time of six months to a year. Unfortunately, within the last two decades or perhaps longer than that, many traditional, "old school" dojo instructors that became frustrated realizing how nowadays our kids are growing up, have been gradually changing their approach to teaching, pulling away from the traditional, old ways to the newer "McDojo," easier approach, in order to keep their dojo open, making the problem even worse. Through the last two decades, many traditional instructors have shared with me that if they teach their students the way that they learned the traditional Arts, they would not have any students at all. The common complaint is that our kids are not tough anymore and that they are not willing to work hard, so instead of discouraging them and losing them as paying students, instructors have "modified" their curriculum to keep students happy at their dojo.

I can see their point of view and understand their frustration and why they do that, but if we all take that approach, what is going to happen to our next generation of budoka (martial arts practitioners)? What can we expect from budo in one or two generations? Those are questions that I keep in my mind on a daily basis; those are questions that have motivated me to choose that subject as the center of this article.

I've also spent the last two decades trying to answer an even more difficult question: What can we do to resolve the problem; what can we do to make sure that dento (traditional) budo has a bright future for the next generations?

Finding the Solution
The intention of this writing is not to focus on the negative of the sad realization of what is happening with our youth, but rather to identify that reality and offer a possible solution to the question, "What can we do to help have a better future for the traditional martial arts?"

Running a traditional, full-time dojo,

the traditional martial arts.

Unfortunately, we have also always had instructors that did not receive the appropriate education to run a dojo where the proper values of the martial arts would be taught, or in other cases the instructors chose deliberately not follow the hard and difficult path to teach the traditional way. The reader will ask the question, "Why would instructors choose to not teach the Arts properly?"

The answer is very simple but very sad. If a traditional instructor chooses to teach the martial arts in the traditional way and he/she enforces at his/her dojo on a daily basis

discipline, respect, dedication, hard work, and old moral values, students will need to dedicate a minimum of six or more years to obtain their Shodan (first-degree black-belt). In general, in consequence of the many habits described earlier and due to the way that our kids are growing in society, a large majority of kids and young adults will be immediately discouraged from joining that dojo, or they will quit shortly after joining.

As a natural alternative, those potential students of a more "modern mentality" will find their way to one of the so-called "McDojo," schools that in contrast will be focusing on

A group of the dedicated teenagers, core of the Bushikan Mentor Program, with Shorin Ryu instructor Tajima Kazuo Sensei in Okinawa during one of the training sessions in our annual trip, August 2018.

in probably one of the most difficult places in the USA (such as California is), has allowed me to see and experience firsthand what is happening with our modern society and to easily come out with a forecast of what future budo can become if we do not do something drastic now. One of the delicate subjects around the world nowadays is a topic that many people do not want to talk about or choose to ignore for convenience: the issue of Global Warming. Experts have been pin pointing for many years that if we do not do something to control it now, soon it is going to become irreversible. Please understand that this statement about Global Warming has nothing to do with politics; it is just a subject that I am bringing up as a point of comparison. This article has no political connotations.

Well, in a similar fashion, I strongly believe that the future of the traditional martial arts is headed in the same direction. I am not even going back to the days when some of the influential instructors shaped some of the traditional ryu-ha (schools/styles) that we can find nowadays around the world. In the case of karate alone, instructors such as Higaonna Kanryo Sensei from Goju Ryu, Itosu Anko Sensei from Shorin Ryu, Uechi Kanbun Sensei from Uechi Ryu, in between many other influential instructors from that era or even before them. Just from the early 1970s when I initiated my journey in

budo to today, things have changed so much that for me it is very hard and difficult to accept it.

It is cheap and easy to complain, to point a finger at a problem, but it is difficult and hard to work on a solution. I have always lived my life considering that if I see a problem and I do not do anything to fix it, I am a part of the problem. I always like to think of the simple fact of life that if we plant a young, small, five-gallon tree and stake it, that tree will grow straight and more than likely healthy. On the other hand, if we do not stake that tree more than likely it will grow crooked. With that thought in mind, I like to think that children are not too different from that tree. If we raise a child with good moral values and habits, that child more than likely is going to grow following that pattern, but if we raise the same child with no moral values and bad habits more than likely that child will grow having a poor foundation and because of that more than likely will not have a strong outlook in life.

What does all this have to do with the future of the traditional martial arts practitioners? The answer is, a lot.

If a dojo instructor receives a new student that from day one is complaining about all the difficult aspects of the classes, the instructor has two main options depending of his/her beliefs. If the instructor believes in the old school values,

he/she will do his/her utmost to try to guide and change that child to become a traditional practitioner; an approach that more than likely will require lots of work and perseverance.

In the other option, the instructor will make it easy on himself /herself, directing his/her approach toward keeping that child at the dojo "happy," and letting him/her get away with all his/her complaints.

I am, personally, an old school practitioner. But I also believe that kids are the future in every single sense of the word—in society and in budo—so because of that, I believe that we should work hard to help them. Even now, after 49 years of my humble journey in the traditional martial arts, if I receive one of those new students evidently not equipped to understand traditional training, I do not bend my rules and norms even a bit to keep him/her happy at our dojo. I always put in the hard work to try to change that kid in every class that he or she attends, but unfortunately in the back of my mind I always ask myself if that kid will be able to change or not. Going back to the analogy of the tree, I wonder if I will be able to straighten out that tree (that child), how settled is that tree in his/her growth, how capable is that child of changing to learn better habits? Obviously, dealing with brand new adult students is even more difficult, because now we are talking about a "full grown tree" with very settled ways and habits.

Once that I came to this important realization, I had to make an important decision: Should I continue doing my job, wondering if I would be able to change those kids that lack the tools to become traditional martial arts practitioners or, should I try to find a better solution? The option to turn our dojo into another of those McDojo where children dictate the rules never has been nor ever will be an option.

After making the conscientious decision to take the hard road to work on creating and/or changing kids to be traditional practitioners, hopefully to become the next generation of traditional practitioners, the main question was how to accomplish that difficult task? The answer was to start to plant as many "young, five-gallon trees" as possible!

Plan in Action

My plan was to have a campaign to start teaching as many young kids as possible, as young as possible, with the mission hopefully to train enough of those kids with good, "old school" habits, so as they grew up, they wouldn't be different from the old days. The goal was that those kids

would become the essence of our dojo, the future adults at the dojo if they continued training, and even better the foundation of a new generation of traditional martial artists.

To accomplish this task (that from the beginning I knew was not going to be easy), in additional to already teaching at our dojo young students from three years old, in February 1993 I started our special Day Care Program at a daycare center across the street from our dojo. The program involved twice per week picking up the whole kindergarten class from the daycare center, teaching them how to cross the street as a group, and then taking them to our dojo to have a traditional karate class for one hour. The group would learn proper Japanese terminology, traditional protocol of reigi (manners ceremony), kihon (basic techniques), and depending on the maturity of the group they also would learn kata (forms). The group that was four to five years old would be engaged in class year-round. The principal of the center and the teachers were so impressed from the beginning of the changes in those young martial artists that we ran our program uninterrupted

from February 1993 until March 2020 when the Corona Virus become a problem around the world. The principal has told us that we will be back once the Corona Virus gets under control.

In addition to teaching at the daycare center, in July 1994 I also started to teach karate and self-defense classes through our After School Program at local elementary schools. Since then, we have also taught our program uninterrupted in three or four elementary schools every year through March 2020, when schools limited activities at the school districts due to the Corona Virus.

In 1997 the Superintendent of the Unified San Marcos School District in our area approved our Bushikan Self-Defense Program to be taught at elementary schools of the District. This program, different from the After School Program that we were already teaching in some of the district schools, was designed and approved to be taught during regular school hours. The Superintendent, without being a martial arts practitioner, approved our program because he understood not only the importance of the kids of his district having the opportunity to learn self-defense

Sanguinetti Sensei's team training in Uechi Ryu at Senaga Yoshitsune Sensei's dojo on Okinawa, July 2019. Many of the core of the Bushikan Mentor Program are seated in seiza in front of Senaga Sensei.

skills, but also understanding the positive feedback that our After School Program had already generated from the kids showing good character development through the positive and beneficial values of the Arts.

We ran our Bushikan Self-Defense Program successfully in three elementary schools from 1998 until 2010. We stopped conducting the program because the District made the decision to cancel all programs conducted during school hours. During the 13 years that we conducted the program all the school principals noticed and appreciated the change in attitude and respect of the children that participated.

What Positive Has Come from All These Program?
What have been the benefits of working with all those kids at the schools for so many years? From among many great stories that I have been proud to witness through the years I would like to mention a few:

My own daughter Nicolla started practicing at our dojo at age three, and now at the age of 32 has become not only the student who has been at the dojo the longest, but also one of our instructors.

Kyle Williams started to train with us at age three as a "little rascal" at the Day Care Center. He is now 24 years old and is one of the instructors at our dojo and a role model for kids coming up in the ranks.

Arshiya Zarmahd started to train with us at age six in one of the After School Programs at an elementary school. He is now 18 years old and he is one of our assistant instructors at the dojo and another role model for our kids.

Ryan Swaney started to train with us at age seven in one of our Bushikan Self-Defense Programs at an elementary school. She is now 18 years old and she is one of our assistants at the dojo and a role model for our kids.

What role do these students at our dojo play in the big picture, to make it possible that the next generation of budoka receive and continue with dento budo?

The four students mentioned, in addition to a group of other fine, teenage black-belts that also started at our dojo at a young age and have been training for a good number of years, are the foundation of our Bushikan Mentor Program and are hopefully the future of our organization and the next generation of budoka.

What is the Bushikan Mentor Program?
It is a program that we have developed and implemented already for many years at our dojo, based primarily on those teenagers that have been coming to our dojo directly from an early age, or from our Day Care Program, After School Programs, and Self-Defense Programs that we conducted through the years. The initial goal of the Program was to raise at the dojo a core of students from a very young age exclusively with "old school values," where respect, discipline, hard work, accountability, and respect for their rank and belt were the most important focus of their upbringing. After many years of hard work with that group of students, they became the foundation of our Program. They became the real role models at the dojo, making every new student coming to the dojo understand by example what was expected from them in every single class.

From day one at our humble dojo, and for the benefit of the affiliated dojo that we have around the world, I stress to all our instructors and students that our organization is a Family in every sense of the word. As a Family, we encourage all our Family Members to help each other,

especially higher ranks consistently showing by example to lower ranks, not just when it is convenient. Through our Bushikan Mentor Program on a daily basis in all our classes, we guide, encourage, and hold accountable the role of senpai (senior students), no matter what level or age the students are.

As we recall history, in the early days of karate in Okinawa, neither karate gi (karate uniform) nor obi (belt) existed in training. Later on, in mainland Japan, the founder of judo, Kano Jigoro Sensei, introduced the belt rank system for his judo students. That system consisted of a white-belt for beginners and a black-belt for instructors or advanced students. This innovation by Kano Sensei in mainland Japan was observed and implemented by many Okinawan karate instructors. Beginners would start training at a dojo wearing a plain white-belt and, as the years passed by, when the instructor considered the student to have reached the desirable technical and emotional level, he would award them directly a black-belt.

Over time, many Okinawan karate instructors came to the realization that sometimes students would quit their training because it was a long time from when they started their training wearing a white-belt until the point that they were recognized for their many years of hard work by being awarded a black-belt. This observation brought a modification to the initial, two-tier belt system that

Bushikan Mentor Program in action. Different mentors work on different material, depending on what the mentee needs.

Training Okinawan Goju Ryu at Gibo Seiki Sensei's dojo, Gibo Sensei demonstrates bunkai with one of the core teenagers of the Bushikan Mentor Program.

established the levels of mudansha (persons that do not hold a Dan or black-belt rank) and yudansha (persons that hold a Dan or black-belt rank). Mudansha practitioners would start their training with a white-belt and, as they progressed, they would be awarded in order of hierarchy with belts colored yellow, green, and brown. Finally, they would reach the level of yudansha and therefore be awarded with black-belt rank. At our dojo we follow the belt system initially implemented in Okinawa.

Every instructor running a dojo has the power to decide how and what they teach, regarding not only the technical aspects of the Arts at their dojo, but also how they award belts and in general what type of message they want to send to the students and parents at their dojo on a daily basis. This is what becomes the Culture of the Dojo.

The Culture of the Dojo is basically the stamp, the signature, the message that the owner of each dojo sends to his/her community. Often people that do not know me, ask me the question, "Who is your competition in your area?" I always surprise those inquisitors telling them no one, even though I have a "McDojo" literally around the corner from us. My explanation is very simple: They do not have the same "Culture" that we have at our dojo.

Sad to say, part of the Culture of those McDojo is that in order to keep their students (mostly kids) happy,

they have double and sometime triple the number of mudansha ranks to award more belts and obviously sell them to parents, thereby profiting from them. Supporters of that "rainbow belt system" often argue, "What is wrong with offering many belts to the kids if it keeps them engaged?" A lot, and to me that is part of the problem that we are having with our kids not growing up with a strong foundation to be the future of budo.

Why is that? Because if we want to see it and accept or not, for those kids the belt doesn't mean anything anymore. Teaching for over 25 years at several elementary schools has given me the opportunity to interact with many kids that approach me during my classes to let me know that they are also practitioners of the Arts. On average, most mudansha practitioners can't tell me the next color belt they will obtain, or even the order of all the belts in their dojo, because they have so many. Probably the most noticeable are the black-belts that when seeing me at the school wearing my karate gi with my kuro obi (black-belt) make the point to approach me to quickly to make sure I know they are also black-belts as they are wearing street clothes at their schools. Most of them, who are 10 years old or younger, tell me that have obtained their belts on an average of one or two years of training. I never discourage or talk down to them, because it is not their

fault that their instructors have not instilled a proper Dojo Culture in them.

The reader will say, "Why is this person is so concerned about the belts? They are just tools to keep the kids engaged in their training." The problem is that we are not realizing that we are giving superficial belts to our "future of budo," but more importantly we are not attributing any accountability to those belts, resulting in a final consequence that nowadays becoming a black-belt has almost no meaning behind it.

As a natural result, becoming a sensei does not mean anything either, because most of those McDojo not only award their black-belts in one to two years or less—with who knows how much meaningful training—but also most of those "black-belts" are immediately being named sensei at their dojo. As it snowballs, since now being a sensei is very common and easy to obtain, to establish a noticeable difference we find in the martial arts titles such as Master, Grand Master, Grand-Grand Master, Professor in the Martial Arts, and even a religious title as Reverend in the Martial Arts.

What Makes Our Bushikan Mentor Program a Success?

From day one, any new student attending our classes is educated in the simple but powerful concept that I have the expectation of everyone to do their best in class. The higher the student's rank, the higher their responsibility of showing by example and acting as a role model and a leader helping others during class. That sense of role model and leader or senpai is something that we teach not only through our daily interaction with our students during classes, but more importantly it gets engraved in our students' minds when they start to earn their ranks. At our dojo every single rank is important and it is treated with the utmost respect and attention.

As I mentioned before, at our dojo we follow the initial, five-color belt system implemented in Okinawa, which in order are white, yellow, green, brown and black; not making any distinction between children or adults. In between those color belts, depending on their kyu (ranks before black-belt) our students receive at the tip of their obi one black stripe (ippon

sen) or two, little black stripes (nihon sen).

Every student under 18 years old, no matter what rank they have, once they have earned the right to test due to their consistent, good technical performance, proper reigi, and in upper levels demonstration of leadership, they will also need to get written approval from their parents and teachers at school. Obtaining this approval is intended to emphasize the need to do what is expected of them at home and at school. The message to our youngsters is that in order to test at our dojo they not only need to do a great job at the dojo but equally importantly they need to do an excellent job at home and at school.

To reinforce the importance of ranks awarded at our dojo, especially considering that our students in their whole journey in budo can only obtain four, colored belts, we have a procedure that involves a ceremony where we involve the parents of our children testing. As the high point of the ceremony, I put every single new belt on the student in seiza (kneeling position), making a serious remark of the importance of the new belt obtained, making it clear to the student that with the new rank not only am I going to expect more from him/her in and outside the dojo, but his/her parent and teacher will also.

From then on, in every class I hold those new ranks to the maximum expectations at all times at the dojo, from performing at the best technical level, to helping others, to acting as a role model during classes. It is extremely rare at our dojo that we need to call to the attention of any of our color belts that they are not doing what is expected from them during class. If a complaint from home or from school is brought to my attention from any of our students, the same day in class I make the entire student body line up and kneel down in seiza position. I call the student in question to the front of the whole class and I do not need to do more than ask him/her two simple questions: "Who put your belt on you?" And, "What did I ask you before I put that belt on you?" There are no questions or doubts in their minds; all immediately answer that I was the one that took his time to honor their new rank, putting their belts on, and that I asked them if they were ready to honor those new belts. The common consensus among our students is that I ask them the question 10,000 times because I really make a big deal of my expectations.

The children's parents play a very important role in helping me to solidify the important concept of not only honoring those new belts but also keeping their word to me by instilling a new set of values in their kids by holding them accountable at home. I love it when once in a while some of our parents share with me that sometimes when their kids have one of those days at home that they decide to test their parents' patience, the parent does not need to do more than ask them if they want for me to know of their behavior for them to return to a good behavior immediately.

One of my favorite stories is the case of our little five-year-old Sofia, some years back, that would often test her parents' patience. One particular weekend she put all her best effort into driving her parents insane. By Sunday her Dad told her that he was completely fed up with her horrible behavior so on Monday he was going to let me know of her attitude. Little Sofia did not think twice and immediately replied to Dad that she would prefer to get a spanking instead of her behavior being reported to me. Mom still reported little Sofia's unacceptable behavior to me the next day and it was the last time the she challenged Mom's and Dad's patience.

I said that "I love it" when that happens because, like Sofia's parents, other parents tell me that it is not that their children are afraid of me, it is that they don't want to disappoint me. Our children have it very clear in their minds that I laugh and play with them when it is the proper moment, but at the same time they know that I have no tolerance nor accept excuses when they do not live up to the expectations that I hold them responsible for.

What is very neat to me is that our kids are still kids; this means that they come to our dojo to enjoy and laugh, but they know that when it is time to work out and follow directions, they take their role very seriously during our classes. I strongly believe that kids not only crave boundaries in their lives, but also they really enjoy responsibilities because it gives them a sense of accomplishment and pride.

How Do We Apply the Bushikan Mentor Program?

At our dojo all classes are taught primarily by me and/or by my right hand in life, Chrisan Sensei. If the need arises, we will ask one of the other instructors to fill-in with teaching duties. As we get into the description of our Bushikan Mentor Program we like to think of the simple concept of the natural configuration of a pyramid, where Chrisan Sensei and I are at the top directing the flow within the structure. Just under us we place our adult black-belts with the

Yondan and Sandan Black Belt members of the Bushikan Mentor Program working with Sanguinetti Sensei on Kururunfa kata.

ranks of Yondan (4th Degree) and Sandan (3rd Degree) that hold the important position of top Mentors at the dojo. As Mentors they will have one to three adult or junior (teenager) black-belts ranked Shodan (1st Degree) or Nidan (2nd Degree) directly underneath them assigned as a Mentee. In exchange those adult or teenage black-belts will also serve as Mentors, having one to three brown-belts or green-belts directly underneath them assigned as a Mentee.

The role of Mentor at our dojo is a serious designation of responsibility, and not just a "babysitting title" for us the instructors to get a break during our classes. On the contrary, it is more work for us as instructors because when the time comes for Mentors to work with their Mentee, we the instructors have to make sure that they are on the right path of mentoring. The rules are that the Mentor has to show by example whatever the mentee is working on. If the Mentee is practicing kihon, the Mentor has to execute the same number of repetitions as his/her Mentee, but faster and stronger. If the Mentee is practicing kata, the Mentor has to execute the same kata in front of the Mentee but in a "mirrored" form, not only to watch at all times the correct execution of the kata, but equally importantly for the Mentor to grow technically by executing the kata backwards.

Our Mentor Program is designed for both the Mentor and the Mentee to grow and improve. When I grew up in the martial arts, like most instructors, no one taught me how to become an instructor. I learned on my own from watching, paying attention to other instructors, and experiencing. Our Bushikan Mentor Program is designed to educate our students to become instructors; our Bushikan Mentor Program is designed with the goal that our current teenage black-belts pass on to the next group of students coming behind them what it takes to become "an old school practitioner."

On a regular basis during the week, all our junior teenage black-belts and some of our junior teenage brown-belts have to come at least once per week to our kid's classes to help; not to teach. Through these classes Chrisan Sensei and I give these black and brown-belts tips on how to help the kids during classes.

On Saturdays we have a mixed class where adults and kids, black, brown and green-belts attend by invitation only. Even though the official time to start the class is at 10:30 a.m., all our students show up at the dojo between 8:30 and 8:45 a.m. to start to workout at 9:00 a.m. until 10:30 a.m. when the regular class starts. The main goal is to have a solid one and one-half hours before the regular class starts where all the Mentors will have the opportunity to work on any material they feel their Mentees will benefit from working on. To me it is very rewarding to see all the Mentors taking pride in helping their fellow doshi to improve, but what is extra rewarding is to see that after so many years of working with these now teenage or young adult black-belts they do not know anything different than to be a practitioner of traditional martial arts of the "old school," and now they are passing that mentality on to the brown and green-belts coming behind them.

One of my greatest satisfactions has been to receive comments from Okinawan instructors paying compliments to our teenagers training with good spirit in the middle of summer in Okinawa, where the extreme heat and humidity defeat many foreigners who are not accustomed to it. All our teenage black-belts and some of our teenage brown-belts have traveled with me to train in Okinawa—some of them more than once.

This year, we have four teenage black-belts graduating from high school. At the moment they don't know if they will leave the area to attend college, so consequently we don't know if we will lose these Mentors or not, but as it is our group of Mentors is preparing three teenage brown-belts to test for Shodan by the time the other four will be graduating. As the Program works those three new Shodan will take the place of the ones graduating if they move out of town, continuing with the "planting of more young trees" to hopefully bring the "old school" to the next generation. ☺

Author Information
Franco Sangunetti
fs@bushikan.com
http://www.Bushikan.com

Developing the Powerful
(Effective) Technical Punch

By Peter Ciecwierz Polander

Hands of the White Eagle Okinawan Kempo

I am sure you have heard many people say in martial arts training, that defense is offense, but what does it really mean? My understanding is that it means to use your defensive moves as offense by converting blocks into atemi strikes. So, how does a serious martial artist train to develop this kind of defense/offense and a technical, effective punch? I have over 50 years of experience practicing different styles of martial arts and I have seen and investigated many ways to train this. In this article I will explain to you, as best I can, how I train and how I teach my students.

All my life I have studied many forms of fighting. These include boxing, Kyokushinkai and Shotokan karate, judo, and jujutsu, to name a few. After emigrating from Poland to the U.S. in 1984 I became an instructor of a martial arts program at Georgetown University in Washington, D.C, and later at the National Institutes of Health in Bethesda, Maryland, the Naval Academy in Annapolis, Maryland, and the National Naval Medical Center in Bethesda, Maryland (now known as the Walter Reed National Military Medical Center). I taught many students in the military and Special Forces, as well as members of the FBI, CIA, and Secret Service. Even though I had good fighting skills, I was still looking for more. I saw many martial arts practitioners who claimed to be masters here in the USA. They were great tournament fighters but none, in my view, were true Masters.

It took me five years to find someone who had trained in the old ways of martial arts and had the ancient knowledge passed down from generation to generation. That person was Taika Seiyu Oyata. I fell in love with his knowledge and personality. He was a warrior that embodied the spirit of true, life protection arts from Okinawa. In 1989 I became a student of Taika Oyata. Over the years he guided me in how to research movements and techniques hidden in the kata. He taught me body mechanics as well as applications of techniques and constantly challenged

me mentally and physically as a martial artist. In 1995 I opened my own dojo in downtown Bethesda, Maryland, under Taika Oyata's Association, RyuTe®. Since he passed away, I started my own association, called the International Okinawan Kempo Federation.

Over the years Taika shared the history of his family and of Okinawa with me, both during seminars and personally, one on one. He told me that in the past, his family and his instructors were entrusted with protection of the Okinawa Royalty (when Okinawa had sovereignty and its own King) for more than 500 years. Oyata came from a samurai family descended from Zana Oyakata of the traditional warrior class. His ancestors became well known when they were advising and protecting the RyuKyu King, Sho Nei, who ruled from 1564–1620. When Satsuma, a powerful Daimyo of the time, invaded Okinawa

Even though I had good fighting skills, I was still looking for more.

in 1609, the Okinawan king was forced to flee to Edo, now known as Tokyo, for his own safety. When the king returned in 1611, he had to formally sign an agreement stating the specific conditions of his return. He and his advisors were told that they had to sign it even though it was demeaning, and to them, dishonorable. They were morally humiliated when they were forced to pledge loyalty to Satsuma over and above their loyalty to the king. All Sho Nei's officials were told to sign this agreement. However, one of the king's men refused to sign it, and that man was Teido Jana Oyakata. After refusing to sign he was taken aside and beheaded. As further punishment,

the Oyakata family name was changed to Oyata which has a double meaning in Japanese and can also be read as shin da, or death. However, this heroic event earned the respect of the warrior class in the RyuKyu Kingdom.

I also came to learn that Oyata's heritage was the only reason that two bushi (warriors) accepted him as their personal student. They would have refused to even look at him if he did not have that heritage. According to old Japanese tradition, instructors rarely teach a family art outside of the family, but if they do it is only ever to those in the same, warrior class. One of these men, Uhugusuku no Tanmei, was in his 90s when Oyata met him and was well known in the region, especially for the distinction of wearing the traditional top knot hair style. The other warrior, Wakinaguni no Tanmei, was of Chinese descent and strongly built. He was also well known for not having fingernails since they had been worn away after striking trees and coral reefs as part of his training. Both instructors taught Oyata the old way of karate. This was not sport, but life protection arts tested on a battlefield.

Before they passed away, the two masters recommended that Seiyu Oyata join the Shigeru Namura's dojo. They believed that the forms Sensei Nakamura was teaching, were the closest to the ones the old Okinawan warriors practiced. When I learned these stories, I knew that Oyata was the master that I had searched for and had hoped to find for so many years. I dedicated myself to learn as much as I could from him and apply as much of his teachings as I could to my own training. I have never seen his equal in application of powerful, 100% effective techniques.

From what I have learned from Taika and from my own investigation, I have developed a training program for a very technical and effective, powerful punch. I would like to share this with you and describe how you can develop it in stages of training. While the concepts I describe are from Taika Oyata, who learned from these two masters, years of study and practice on my own have led me to develop these stages of technical training. Besides stances and tai-sabaki (the concept of body control or body movement), the development of an effective punch is extremely important. I am going to share with you the different stages that I teach to all my senior instructors in America and Europe. It is especially important to take the proper amount of time and start from the beginning to develop and practice each stage appropriately.

Taika Oyata compared this concept of training to the development of a child. He said that first an infant must develop body strength by lifting its head, arms, and legs. When the body is strong enough the child can sit up and then crawl. Next, a child starts using its legs and arms to help it stand up. When the proper muscle strength and balance are developed the baby can try to walk. But it still cannot run! As Taika Oyata said, the basic kata will let you "walk" but the advanced version of kata will let you "run." Development of a strong, technical punch is similar.

Before we get into the technical training, let us discuss building some foundations that should be trained continuously. Conditioning of the fists and strengthening of the wrists are necessary to develop a strong punch. This is achieved by heavy bag and makiwara training and knuckle push-ups. It is a good idea to do these exercises in every training session. In addition, it is essential to develop proper breathing techniques. Never hold your breath while punching. Maintain fifty-percent lung capacity during the beginning of the punch, exhaling to five-percent at the end of the punch. Make sure to have awareness of your breath when you are doing repetitions of punches—this also helps you to focus your energy on your target and conditions your core muscles in a dynamic way.

Stage 1:

In the first stage, a beginner learns how to make a fist. Start with bending and squeezing your fingers into the palm of your hand one by one, with the pinky finger first and ending on the thumb. In this wave like motion, you should feel that you are pushing out all the air from the palm of your hand. Start with the basics by standing in yoi and have your left hand extended forward and right hand

Stage

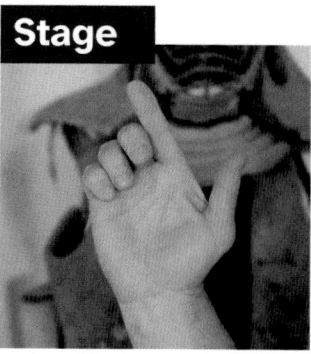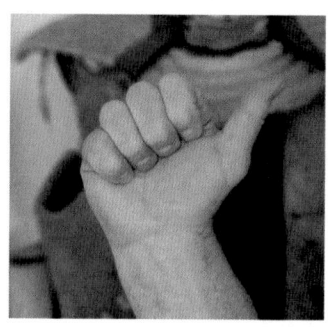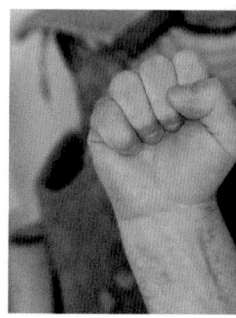

chambered on the right side of your body (gedan- tsuki).

From the gedan-tsuki position there are two main points that must be trained:

1.A When you chamber your right arm to the side of your body, with the elbow bent and your fist palm-up, you are forcing the elbow to be connected to the frame of the body. This prevents you from forming a "chicken wing" position, with the elbow jutting out, which is a weakness—it gives your opponent a possible opening for an arm-bar attack. Your left fist is facing down, with no angle. When striking in this basic form your focus in the punching motion is to wait until the

last moment to finish twisting both fists. After 5,000 of these types of punches you can start the next phase.

1.B Now relax your fists a little, allowing a small space between the fingers and the base of the palm, big enough to place a chopstick or pencil in the space. From a kiba-dachi stance, as you strike, squeeze the fists and eliminate this space as you twist and extend your arm to punch, but only at the last moment of the movement. This added exercise will give you the foundation to develop flow of the positive and the negative energy of the fists while punching. After 5,000 times you are ready for stage 2.

Stage 2:

Next, we need to talk about the defense in the punch. To do this, I need to give you a little bit of background. One time Taika Oyata asked me, "Peter, which is more important: defense or offense?" I hesitated to answer, knowing that his questions were always intended to make you think more deeply about how to train and improve yourself. Finally, he answered for me. He said, "Defense." He explained that if you have a weak defense you may not

have a chance for offense. This answer was so simple, but it really changed my concept of how to train and how I move to make my defense stronger. To start training defense and offense you need to develop a foundation in the following way. Extend your left arm forward and in the moment of extending your right arm to punch, the left arm pulls back and bends and must cross the center line of your body before it is chambered on the left side of your body. In the moment of crossing the center line the left fist needs to face up (knuckles down) and strikes forward across an opponent's attacking arm to the base of their biceps, at the point where it is closest to the elbow. The punch should be delivered as a whipping motion with a recoil back to chamber at the left side of your body. For the strike of the left hand to be most impactful you start by striking with the knuckle bone of the pinky finger. As soon as it contacts the biceps, roll the fist forward until finally the pointer finger knuckle is penetrating the muscle. After 5,000 repeats of this strike, you are ready for stage 3.

youtu.be/9iWii9p529M

Stage 3:

Continue developing offense as defense:

Stand in the kiba-dachi position. This time when you are punching with the right arm, the left arm is retreating at the same time. When your right arm is halfway forward, the left fist opens (don't keep it closed like you did in stages 1 and 2) and strikes over the right arm and forward with an open hand, hitting the imaginary target with your palm first,

following through with your fingers. This strike is aimed at the top of the attacker's forearm. Striking this way can also be interpreted as an elbow attack and arm-bar technique. This is done by the right arm holding and twisting the wrist of the attacking arm so that the opponent's elbow faces up, then the left open palm can strike the exposed elbow, breaking it or forcing the opponent down to the ground face first. After 5,000 punches trained this way you are ready for stage 4.

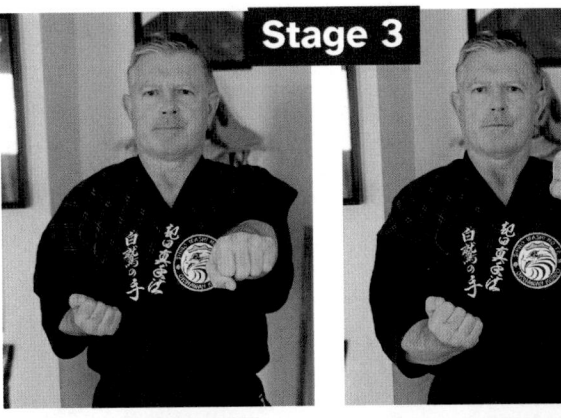

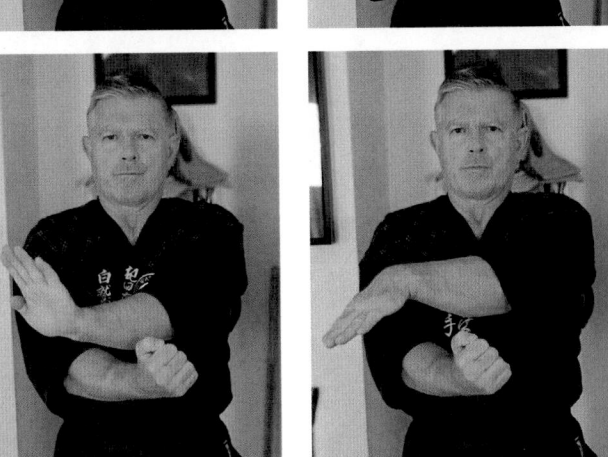

youtu.be/QToJr7AJxw4
youtu.be/w54ucxxijTQ

bugeisha Traditional Martial

Stage 4:

After four years of basic training a student should be ready for study of the shodan punch. To get there, the concepts of how to apply proper angles of the fists and forearms need to be understood.

The impact that angles can have on your technique was taught to me in a very dramatic way that I can never forget. One day when I was having a private session, Sensei Oyata asked me to punch him. As my punch was halfway to hitting him, I experienced tremendous pain in my forearm, which dropped me to the floor. Excruciating pain prevented me from standing up. I thought, "What just happened to me?" Taika Oyata just looked at me and asked me this question: "Did you ever research how your forearm is built? Did you ever take the time to study where the weak spots are? Do you know how to activate them?"

As a 4th degree black-belt at that time, I got extremely excited! To be asking me these kinds of questions meant that my master felt that I reached the level for serious study. He asked me to position my left arm in front of me, bent at a ninety-degree angle, parallel to my stomach. Then he asked me to rotate my thumb up. He told me to take my right arm and place it over my left forearm to make an "X" shape, then to rotate my right fist facing up until it was at a 45-degree angle. He asked me, "Do you see the base of the left arm muscle?" It is in the middle of the forearm. "Strike it!" I did, and right away I had this amazing feeling of electricity and numbing pain running down my arm. All I could think of was, "Wow!" I felt electricity bouncing from my thumb to my forearm muscle and it was intense. But then I remembered how, just a moment ago, Taika caused me so much pain I could not think of anything else.

What I had done to myself was impressive, but it was a level of pain I could take. It was not the level of the pain that dropped me like Taika did. "Taika, can you demonstrate this strike on me again, please?" I asked him. "Punch!!" he said, and I ended up on the floor again! "That was

stupid," I said to myself. It was extremely painful. At that moment I realized that to learn this art (atemi waza) there is nothing like direct application from master to student. You must have it done to you by a master to understand the proper motion and angle and to know the potentially devastating effect it can have. That evening I tried to copy Taika Oyata's strike. I could tell I was getting better at it, but it was still far from what he did.

The following day Taika called me up and asked me, "How many bones do you have in your forearm?"

I answered, "Two."

"Good", he said, and then asked, "What is their shape?"

"They are round," I replied.

"Wrong!" he said. "Now feel your shin bone in your leg. Do you feel the sharp edge of the top of the bone?"

"Yes, sir!" I answered.

Taika Oyata explained that the bones in your forearms are similar. They are oval, not round. If you strike with the sharp side or edge of the bone it is like cutting with the sharp edge of a katana. But there is more to it than just the angle. Part of the strike is also dropping the weight of the body exactly when you connect with the desired striking area of your attacker's body. At that moment you also transfer your energy to the striking area by the movement of your wrist, squeezing and relaxing of the fist and, as a result, creating even more pain. Squeezing of the fist

means the brain is sending a "message" or energy through your body to your opponent. If you keep the fist squeezed tightly, energy is kept in. But when you relax and open your hand the energy flows out and penetrates the area being struck.

When you reach this level of training you should be able to strike multiple points on your attacker's arm. As you extend your punch and continue to strike points on the neck and side of the head of your opponent, it should be in one, fluid motion. You also need to develop vibrating strikes. Please remember that all blocks you study over the years must adjust to become strikes. The best defense is offense. This means in order to make the blocks work, your blocks need to be converted to strikes. Only then are they going to work. Simple, basic blocks are good for basic training, but they are too slow to work in a real fight.

Next, Taika Oyata demonstrated footwork. To train your feet, start again with your left arm forward, and right arm chambered at your side. As you begin the strike with your right arm, raise your right heel slightly. When the right arm is halfway forward, ready to strike down (before striking forward), drop your heel with your body giving weight to the downward strike. As you continue punching forward the right heel raises up as the fist is thrown. This kind of foot work will ensure that the entire body is committed to all aspects of delivering the power of the strike.

youtu.be/wdS-AE5FQUo

Stage 4

Step 5:

Training the black-belt strike, 2nd – 7th Dan. When I was researching this stage, I was reminded of the time Taika Oyata asked me, "What is the meaning of karate?"

I answered, "It means 'open hand,'" referring to the literal meaning of the word.

"Yes," he said, "The open hand is a symbol of peace and also of Okinawan karate. When you look at the open hand it relaxes you. It stands for friendship, honesty. The symbol of the fist scares you. It is a symbol of anger, hatred."

Sometimes modern martial arts teach you a dark side of self-defense, brutalizing it. The old way teaches you the art of balance through character development, which will influence your self-defense and entire lifestyle.

"This is our Guiding Principle Four," he said, "Strive to be a warrior for the construction of a peaceful and free world through the character-building morality and spirituality obtained by learning way of karate."

Then he opened his hand and he described that there are two areas of the palm of the hand. He said that there is a line between the pointer finger and the middle finger dividing the hand into two parts. One part is the thumb and pointer finger area and when you squeeze them you create negative energy. This energy gives you speed. When you squeeze the other fingers in the part that has the middle, ring, and pinky fingers, this energy converts to power and positive energy. When the fist is chambered on the side of your body, squeeze the thumb and pointer finger to generate added

speed to the punch as it is thrown. Reverse this as you extend to punch and, at the very end press and squeeze the middle, ring, and pinky together to increase the power delivered. Once contact is made, open the hand so that the energy can be released and transferred to the target.

To train the black-belt punch, position yourself again with your left

You hold your fist as if it were the hammer and your desired striking area is the nail.

arm extended forward, but make sure that your fist is turned at a 45-degree angle so that your thumb is facing slightly up. Your right arm should be connected to the stomach area this time (not chambered to the side) and more to the center of your body. Your elbow remains connected to your side to prevent being at a weaker angle. Your pinky finger is in line with the center line of your body at the level of the solar plexus. Now, twist your right wrist at a slight angle forward. To check if you have the correct alignment and angles, extend your pointer finger forward. If you are pointing straight to where your opponent would be, or if you are looking in the mirror, straight at your own solar plexus, then you are in the correct position.

From here begin the punch with your right arm and at the same time gently press your thumb and base of your pointer finger together. Your middle,

ring, and pinky fingers stay relaxed. Simultaneously, retract your left arm, pressing the middle, ring, and pinky fingers together and gently squeezing them toward the palm of your hand.

When the elbow of your right arm is "free" (in front of the stomach), strike down across your center line. As your right arm rebounds from this downward strike, turn and strike with your left arm across your right arm, and down and forward in front of your right arm. Then recoil back "inside" at the space between your right arm and solar plexus.

For this to be effective you must strike with the ulna bone of your forearm, then with your knuckles, bending the fist at a downward angle. You accomplish three strikes in one move, once you have practiced many times. As you deliver these strikes you drop your weight and energy simultaneously with the strike, to create a more effective defense/ offense. Do not forget to include the previously explained footwork. As you extend your right arm and as the pinky finger knuckle connects to your opponent's body, your body reacts by going up with it and bringing your body weight and energy behind it. Strikes three, four, and five are done with the movement of your wrist.

Only when you focus with delivering the punch at the 45-degree angle will you be able to do all these strikes in one motion. Taika Oyata compared this with hitting a nail with a hammer. You hold your fist as if it were the hammer and your desired striking area is the nail. These three strikes are applied in this order; #3 is your pinky knuckle touching the striking point first, making a connection to

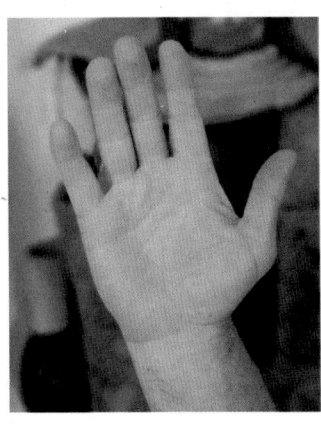 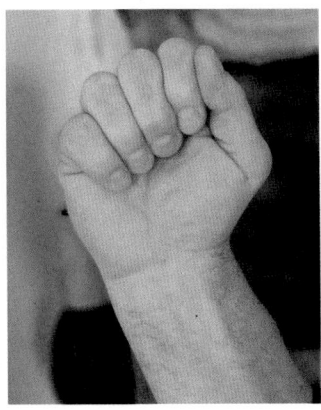 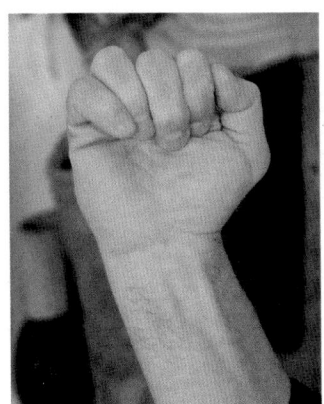 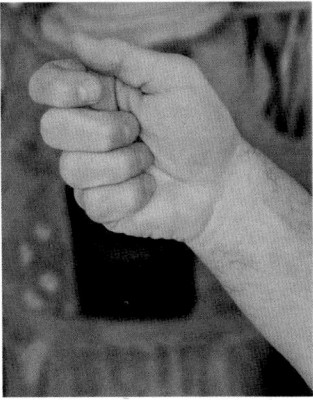

your fist when it is at a 45-degree angle; strike #4 is when your knuckles connect at the 90-degree angle; and then #5 is a penetrating hit at a downward, 45-degree angle. This is when you squeeze your middle, ring, and pinky fingers (in that order) and then penetrate with the pointer finger knuckle. The last thing is to relax and open your hand slightly, releasing built-up energy.

The last stage of development of the effective, technical strike is gaining knowledge of striking blood vessels, vital

Stage 5

youtu.be/ClEYu0hK_3w

points, angles, and proper shaping of the palm to activate them. This knowledge I will pass down only to my senior students.

If you would like to explore the ancient bunkai, kata, and applications, please join our online Saturday classes. For more information, please write or call my cell phone.

Author Information
Peter Ciecwierz Polander
peter.polander@gmail.com
240-305-4040
https://polanderkempo.com

A special thank to Dr. Niamh Cawley and Helen Cawley for their valuable input in this article.

Taika Oyata teaching the two-inch punch "hammer fist

HANDS OF OKINAWA SEMINAR

RYUKYU TE

- GOJU RYU
- MOTOBU RYU
- OKINAWAN KEMPO
- OKINAWAN KOBUDO
- RYU TE
- SHORIN RYU
- UECHI RYU

Open to all styles!
No experience necessary.

12 high ranking, knowledgeable instructors!

Different class taught every hour.

When:
Saturday, October 2nd, 2021
9:00am to 6:00pm
Sunday, October 3rd, 2021
9:00am to 1:00pm

Where:
The Westin
Tysons Corner
7801 Leesburg Pike
Falls Church, VA

The cost:
Saturday $100
Sat. + Sun. $150
($175 at the door)

Contact:
Hanshi Peter Polander
240 305 4040
peter.polander@gmail.com
www.polanderkempo.com

GM S. L. MARTIN
Lineage Holder White Crane Fist
6th Dan Shorin Ryu

DOUG PERRY
Hanshi, 10th Dan
Shorin Ryu

BRUCE HEILMAN
Hanshi, 10th Dan
Okinawa Kenpo
Odo Lineage

GREG LINDQUIST
Hanshi, 10th Dan
ZKKR
Oyakata Kobujitsu

LUIS MORALES
Hanshi, 10th Dan
Okinawa
Goju-Ryu Kenshikai

ROBERT TELLER
Hanshi, 9th Dan
Ryu Shin Kan
Oyata Shin Shu Ho

PETER CARBONE
Hanshi, 9th Dan
Weapons
Preservation Society

PETER POLANDER
Hanshi, 9th Dan
Okinawan Kempo
Oyata Shin Shu Ho

JOHN CARRIA
Hanshi, 9th Dan
Uechi Ryu

GERARD SENESE
Kyoshi, 8th Dan
Oyata Shin Shu Ho

NESTOR FOLTA
Kyoshi, 8th Dan
Uechi Ryu

VERNON JOHNSON
Kyoshi, 7th Dan
Ryu Te; Oyata Shin Shu Ho

A Journey of a lifetime

"A journey of a thousand miles starts with a single step" Lau Tzu

By Marilyn Fierro

I think we are often placed in a position that we did not initially seek because it is where we were meant to be. Certainly, karate was never on my mind when, as a young mother of two, I accidentally discovered it through a self-defense program in a local health club. Little did I know I would eventually make it my life's path.

I found myself totally immersed in my training and traveling to seminars across the country. I was fortunate to have a Sensei who encouraged my enthusiasm and supported me in every way. Hanshi Nick Adler is one of a kind, tough in his teaching yet at the same time offering ways to grow and perfect. He does not produce carbon copies of himself but independent martial artists who develop the skills to grown on their own.

I began to develop my "Attack Prevention" program, which eventually became part of 11 high schools on

Long Island and the subject of several television shows. Additionally, I gained the opportunity to teach these concepts of "Victor Not Victim" through both magazine and Newspaper stories highlighting the success of this program. Recognition and awards followed the various achievements. As my Sensei once said, "If you want to know Marilyn Fierro look up the word 'Perseverance.'"

In 1997 I began the Taking Charge tlevision shows, which gave me the opportunity to film many subjects, but my favorite being martial arts, no matter what the style. Through this medium I was able to film the Okinawan Masters Tour, first in Washington, DC, and then in Atlanta, Georgia.

Sensei Adler and I visited Okinawa in 1991 for the Pre-World Tournament, in 1995 returned to participate with Grandmaster Uezu at the Convention

1997 Editing Taking Charge TV shows at Cable.

Center for a Masters Demonstration, and finally returned to Okinawa in 2007 with my student Rita to again visit with Grandmaster Uezu and this time with Grandmaster Zempo Shimabukuro.

After 20 or more years of keeping notes from a variety of momentous happenings in my karate life I eventually wrote a book called, The Limitless Spirit of the Martial Arts, the

Gravesite of Isshinryu Founder Tatsuo Shimabuku.

title loosely based on my first magazine story about discovering the spirit of the martial arts while training the physical. At each stage of my life, I would think what could be better? Where do I go next? Suddenly a new opportunity would appear.

By 2014 Sensei Adler had received his second recognition of 10th Dan from Grandmaster Uezu, having first received the same recognition in the United States from Grandmaster Harold Mitchum. Soon after, Sensei and I were invited to teach in Thunder Bay, Ontario, by the host, Susan Baldassi. The event was to honor our good friend Hanshi Albert Mady for 30 years of teaching seminars in Canada. This was the first time I would also be a keynote instructor. The event was well organized and the students ready to learn, which always makes teaching easy even when the subject is not. It was a totally enjoyable experience. A local newspaper came and Susan directed the reporter to my seminar. A photo was taken and appeared in the sports section the following day. That first evening however, there was a banquet where we received a certificate for teaching there. Sensei Adler stood and asked if he could speak. I thought it would be about Hanshi Mady but instead he spoke about me. I truly wondered if someone had complained about my classes but he then promoted me to 9th Dan. It took my breath away I could not respond; I

could not even stand up to thank him. When he came back to his seat and I stood to thank him he said look around. There was a standing ovation. What could ever be better than that?

I tell you all of this to bring you to a more current point in my life. We never know what can happen, even when we think nothing can be better than where we are today. We all have ups and downs—it is how we handle them that defines us as who we have become. To me, if you love what you do and do what you love you can't go wrong.

An Offer Too Good to Refuse

Sometime toward the end of October 2019 I received an email from the Okinawan Kaikan asking me if I would be interested in putting my name on a list of high-level black-belts to go to Okinawa and represent both Isshinryu Karate and the USA? The letter, sent from Miguel Da Luz stated that Tsuyoshi Uechi Sensei had recommended me to represent Isshinryu Karate and to let them know if I was interested.

It took my breath away just to receive this invitation. Having been accepted as the highest-ranked woman in Isshinryu Karate at 9th Dan by most Isshinryu Associations, it still amazed me to be considered among so many highly-ranked men here in the USA. Still, I could not refuse the request to be on that list. What a huge honor to even be considered. I

thought about the possibility of being selected and if indeed I was able to make the journey and be part of something so very special. I love Okinawa and the people there so the idea of being able to return was immensely enticing. I had never traveled alone to a foreign country and wondered how I would fare, if selected.

Several weeks later the invitation arrived in full. I was to join three other martial artists from three systems and countries for this "Ri" tour in Okinawa: Jamal Measara (Shorin-ryu, Germany), Damien Martin (Goju-ryu, Australia), and Stephane Fauchard (Shotokan/ Kobudo, France). Arrangements were made and I was to leave on December 12, 2019, returning on the 20th. The actual tour ran from December 15th through the 18th, giving me time to rest and tour one more day before returning home.

Sensei Adler was so proud of me and purchased gifts representative of Long Island (where we live) to present to my fellow travelers as well as to Grandmaster Shimabukuro and Master Tsuyoshi Uechi for their part in this invitation. Additionally, several joint gifts were brought for Grandmaster Angi Uezu, whom I planned to visit on one of my free days. Fortunately, thanks to Andy Sloan, who was stationed there, I was able to see Grandmaster Uezu the first day. Thanks to Uehara Sensei, Chief of the Kaikan, I was able to see him once more before returning home.

The Journey Begins

December 12, 2019, I boarded an ANA flight first to Tokyo and then on to Okinawa, arriving late on the 13th. True to his word, Andy was there to meet me with one of Uechi Sensei's students, Byron Austin. They brought me to the famous Dojo Bar to meet some other people and an opportunity to sign the wall. Finding a place was definitely not easy with so many visitors over the years. But now I can prove I was there.

My first full day in Okinawa. Andy picked me up in the morning and we went to Uechi Sensei's dojo to greet him, offer some gifts, and ask if he would like to come with us to visit Uezu Sensei. As it was, he had a class about to begin, so we had to go on without him. We had a wonderful, joyful visit with Uezu Sensei, who was delighted to see me again. He loved the talking picture frame with photos of Hanshi Adler and myself. We spent about 20 minutes speaking and visiting. At his request we went on to visit his son Katsuya and the Uezu family who are living in the old dojo above the home. Again, another most pleasant visit before leaving to pay our respects to Grandmaster Tatsuo Shimabuku, the founder of Okinawan Isshinryu Karate. In my past visits it has always been one of the first things we would do before training or demonstrations. After a quick lunch Andy brought me back to the hotel.

I had hoped to connect with Pam and John from Florida, who always go to Okinawa during the same time, but unfortunately, they were tied up with other obligations. It was just as well, since I was still jetlagged and exhausted, so I used the rest of the time to unpack and catch up on my rest.

The following day (December 15th) was supposed to be the start of the tour, but I received the itinerary and realized that it was not going to begin until early the following morning. Finding myself with a free day I thought it prudent to pay a visit to Shuri Castle. There had been a fire and much of it had burned down. Still, it had also been a tradition to visit the castle on each of my former trips to Okinawa. The Novotel hotel is about ½ way to the Castle so I thought I could walk it, but the people at the desk informed me it is a difficult and long walk so I opted for a taxi. Good thing, too, because the walk up the hill to the first steps was already tiring on my knees. I never thought I would make it up the many stone steps with no railing—I was in so much pain. I must have looked a sight because an elderly gentleman walked up to me and offered his hand. How embarrassing, but I took it without hesitation. He and his wife were so kind to me. And no, I did not tell them

Shuri Gate

I was there for a karate tour.

Once on level ground I was able to walk around to view some of the damage to the surrounding buildings. Shuri Castle had suffered other fires and had been rebuilt, leaving no doubt it would be this time as well. Fortunately, the Gate remained, a sign of welcome and the endurance of the people of Okinawa.

Upon return to the hotel, I stopped to pick up something to eat and spotted Jamal Measara from the photo I had seen of him and stopped to say hello. We chatted a bit when he pointed out a man with a Goju-ryu shirt and I thought that it could be Damian Martin, so I called out his name. It was nice to have met two others from the tour. Jamal's

instructor is Grandmaster Zenpo Shimabukuro who was meeting him that evening. I asked the time and made sure to stop back at the lobby to say hello to him and give him some gifts from the States.

The tour was set to start at 8:30 the following morning, when we met and left for the Okinawan Kaikan for orientation. There we were introduced to the representatives of our styles of karate as well as representatives of the Japan Travel Bureau who sponsored the tour. During introductions, Uehara Sensei, Chief of the Kaikan, came out with a copy of my book, The Limitless Spirit of the Martial Arts, to show the masters present photos from my previous visits. They loved seeing people they

Author with Zenpo Shimabukuro

Marilyn Fierro & Tsuyoshi Uechi at the Kaikan.

knew. I then presented them my trading card which has a photo of me taken at a beach during my previous trip to Okinawa. They recognized the beach as White Beach, which I did not know. Uezu Sensei had brought my student, Rita, and I there to take pictures at his favorite beach.

From there we proceeded to the Kaikan for another orientation. At that point I realized there were three groups representing Shu, Ha, Ri (beginner, intermediate, and advanced). Our group was the Ri group. We did not interact again with the other groups until the last day of the tour. I was the only woman in my group, but it was not until that last day that I realized I was the only woman martial artist there. The others were representatives of the media or the tour.

We went to the locker room to change into our uniforms and then returned to the gorgeous training area to meet with our sponsoring instructors. Jamal Measara and Stephan Fauchard trained with Grandmaster Zempo Shimabukuro in Shorin-ryu karate, Damien Martin trained with Tsuneo Kinjo in Goju-ryu Karate, and I trained with Tsuyoshi Uechi in Isshinryu Karate. The session lasted close to two hours of constant training. I am sad to share that my body did not fare well, barefoot on the hard floor. We took photos with our corresponding instructors and returned to the Okinawan Karate Information Center. Here we were

Grandmaster Nakamoto in front of Gate he painted L-R Damien Martin, Stephane Fauchard, Grandmaster Nakamoto, Jamal Measara, Marilyn Fierro.

able to put our shoes back on, which was a great relief for me. An Okinawan lunch of "Karate Soba" was served, an original dish made with boned rib, Okinawan-style stewed pork ribs, and pig's feet. I did remove one joint that looked to me more like a pig's snout.

The tour was a combination of karate and culture, and included a

drive to Ihara, Itoman, where we were able to experience Okinawan Lacquerware making. It was an opportunity to first view a video of how the objects were created and then experience firsthand the creation of a Lacquerware plate. The Lacquerware Sensei went around helping each of us learn the various

Hokoma Sensei with Author and her book..

Monument to Higaonna and Miyagi.

techniques necessary to complete our projects. While the projects were all similar, we each added our own touch to our final achievement. At the end our creations were carefully packaged, along with a stand for display when we returned to our respective homes.

We left there for Naha and Madamichi, via an important road connecting Shurijo Castle with the southern parts of the kingdom. The tour continued along many old roads to view the schools where so many of the founders of Okinawa karate taught a variety of school subjects in addition to pursuing their own karate growth.

In 1994, Hanshi Adler and I had met Grandmaster 10th Dan Masahiro Nakamoto Sensei when he was part of a contingent of masters visiting from Okinawa, so I was thrilled to find myself and our group at his dojo and home of the Okinawa Dento Kobudo Hozon-kai Bumbu-kan honbu. After introductions, we were told not to take any photos of the dojo or Museum. Everything was so well organized and appropriate. Grandmaster Nakamoto is very strong—he works out daily and uses weapons and tools as weights. He handed us something that looked like a sledge hammer with a cement base for each of us to feel. Can you imagine working out with such heavy weight all the time? It is certainly evident when you see his physique.

From the dojo walked up to another

Karate research information center L-R Jamal Measara, Stephane Fauchard, Damien Martin.

level which housed the museum. Any weapon you have ever seen or heard of was there and in a variety of versions. The weapons covered the walls and shelves. In the center of the room were long tables filled with the books he has written, some of which were translated to English by Miguel Da Luz of the Kaikan. I found one that I thought Sensei Adler would like but soon found out there is a time and place for everything. I walked around for a long time holding that book and the 3,000 yen before I was able to actually purchase it. Once downstairs

we were offered tea, fruit, and snacks. We also learned that Nakamoto Sensei was a wonderful artist. He presented each of us with a signed copy of a book with his art work.

Dinner that evening was Shabu Shabu. It is similar to a fondu in that boiling pots of water are set on the table along with a variety of foods which we would pick up with our chopsticks and cook. Several people share the pot so it was important to pay attention that what we put in was what we took out. Such a fun and interesting way to eat. This was

Ryukyu Dancer demonstrating Kobudo.

Damien Martin, & Marilyn Fierro with Ryukyu Dancers.

followed by an excellent display of Ryukyu dancers. Again, a karate connection since many moves have been hidden within the dances. More evidence of this was the Bo (staff) dance, which was indeed a kata performed excellently. We later learned the performer was a student of Shinpo Matayoshi. No wonder she was so good.

The following day we were back at the Kaikan for our last day of training with our sponsors and a photo opportunity as a group with our teachers, outside by a beautiful pavilion which overlooked the ocean. This was followed by lunch at a restaurant close to the Kaikan in Tomigusuku. There we enjoyed conversation with our sponsoring instructors. Uehara Sensei, Chief of the Kaikan, joined Uechi Sensei and myself at one of the tables. A variety of foods were laid out on a long table which acted like a buffet with many changing dishes from which to choose.

We returned to the Kaikan and the Okinawan Karate Information Academy research room and were presented with much information about the founding masters of various styles, where they lived and taught, as well as the efforts to keep the history and legacy of karate alive in Okinawa,

where it is already considered a National Treasure.

We visited the grave site of Chojun Miyagi, the founder of Goju-ryu Karate, and many other places of interest to karate practitioners, including Maeda Kouchi (the "Hacksaw Ridge" in the amazing story of Desmond T. Doss). The group then went on to visit several more

monuments and areas one would never have found without guidance, all related to karate and its history.

Dinner that evening was at "A Taste of Okinawa," where dishes of every kind were placed on the table family style and soon replaced by another and another, from fish of all kinds to meats, including hotdogs and cheeseburgers. Quite a different and

Making Lacquerware.

Conference center at the hotel L - R Jamal Measara, Damien Martin, Stephane Fauchard, Marilyn Fierro, Miguel Da Luz and our guide Asato Oshiro.

very filling experience.

The last day of the tour brought us to the Okinawan Prefectural Budokan for Karate Kaikan Exchange training. There we were greeted by a representative of the Association of Okinawa Motobu Udundi-karate-kobudo. We were brought into the training hall to meet the instructor, Shinsuke Moromizato Sensei. He told us we were to learn an eku (oar) form. After changing into our uniforms, we returned to witness a wonderful demonstration of not only the eku form but also the application of eku against eku. This was done smoothly without touching weapon to weapon. Body mechanics and striking were greatly emphasized. More demonstrations were performed. Oar vs. empty hand, bare hand vs. bare hand with lots of very graceful, flowing moves, and some Tuite were evident in his performance. I have a lot of problems with my shoulders so had to excuse myself from participating in the actual form. But I admit now I do not think it would have been that bad to have tried since the oar seemed

lighter than I expected. There is so much more than I can write in the article. I do suggest if you ever plan to come to Okinawa and train you contact the Kaikan directly and set up this type of training. Our tour was sponsored by a combination of the JTB and the Okinawan Karate Kaikan to bring the tradition and training of karate to all interested martial artists.

It was time to leave for lunch although I would have been just as happy to spend the day with Moromizato Sensei. We had a different type of buffet lunch and then it was off to our next adventure, one that I was hoping for as soon as I knew I would be returning to beautiful Okinawa: a visit to Hokoma Sensei's Okinawan Karate Museum in Nishihara. Matt Apsocardo's book, Tales of the Western Generation, was accepted into the museum and I am among others with a chapter in that book. When the opportunity to return to Okinawa came about there were several things I wanted to do. See Master Angi Uezu again, visit the grave of Isshinryu's founder, Tatsuo

Shimabuku, and finally see if I too could get my book, The Limitless Spirit of the Martial Arts, into the museum.

Hokoma Sensei is genuinely a happy person and seemed to be proud to show off his dojo and wonderful museum collection. So much history, articles, books and weapons and memorabilia. We eventually ended up in a small area and were invited to sit, talk, and have some candy. This was the opportunity for me to ask if he would like the copy of my book that I had been clutching in my arms all this time. He opened the book and saw the photos from my past trip and was so delighted to accept the book. I, of course, was elated.

We had visited many important areas for karate, which included Motobu and Miyagi, but up until this point I did not have an opportunity to show Isshinryu's connection. When I got up and looked around the area we were seated in I noticed the kanji for Isshinryu, the photos with Kichiro Shimabuku (the son of our founder), and a photo of Tatsuo Shimabuku along with Don Nagle and others. I was able to point out that my lineage is Tatsuo Shimabuku to Don Nagle to Nick Adler and then to me. I felt very proud at that moment and my own place in Isshinryu's history. Every day of this tour had been awesome and each day better than the one before.

It was not over yet. We were next scheduled to experience Ryukyu Bingata. We were given a choice of stencils and a small carry bag to work on. The Sensei for this cultural activity taught us what to do and came around helping whenever needed.

We returned to the hotel to get ready for a meeting in the conference hall. This was the first time since our initial introduction that we met with the other groups in this tour. We compared impressions from three different points of view and enjoyed Karate Latte and a Ninja show.

Finally, we were off to a dinner buffet at Izakaya Lio. All three groups were again together and had another opportunity to meet on an individual basis and chat. There were tons of food, beer and wine as well. It was sad to say goodbye to all the friends we made during this time but thankfully some of us have been able to continue our correspondence.

My deep gratitude to Uehara Sensei who offered to bring me back to Hamahiga Island the following day since I was still in Okinawa. He also took me to other historical areas in Okinawa and memorably to Chotoku Kyan's home area and the bridge where he famously took students to practice Naihanchi on the edge of the bridge.

There is so much to write about and not enough space here, but if you are interested in more details and anecdotes from the trip, please see my latest book, The Martial Spirit Continues—The Journey Never Ends, available on Amazon.com.

This is a reminder that we never know what lies ahead. Our journey is ongoing if we keep our eyes open for the next opportunity. ◎

Author Information
Marilyn Fierro
Okinawan Isshinryu Karate
marilyn774@aol.com
https://smithtownkarate.com/

Books to
Inspire and Motivate

by Marilyn Fierro

The Limitless Spirit of the Martial Arts

In the early 1970s Marilyn Fierro found herself pursuing a way of life that was supposed to be closed to women - the martial arts.

Join her as she tells her story of personal growth, spirituality, and achievement (both internally and externally).

The Martial Spirit Continues:
The Journey Never Ends

The book will take the reader through many steps of growth and accomplishment through Martial arts and TV production and achieving goals. Presented along with steps to help make your goals a reality. The author also takes you on a journey to Okinawa representing both the USA and Isshinryu Karate. The journey never ends, if you follow your dreams with a plan and keep taking one step after another on that journey, you will be able to do anything you put your heart to.

Available on
amazon

https://smithtownkarate.com/

Tetsuhiro Hokama

By James Pankiewicz

外間
哲弘

In May 2020, James Pankiewicz and Chris Willson visited Hokama Tetsuhiro sensei to record an in-depth interview on camera for the Sensei series of interviews with Okinawan teachers (www.bujin.tv - for the video series).

Hokama sensei has lived a life immersed in the martial culture of Okinawa since his young childhood. Today he is internationally renowned as one of the leading scholars and practitioners in this field.

In this interview he was unusually open about his recollections of his teachers and the community he grew up in. We felt we had been given some special insights into the characters of the teachers and seniors who molded his path of learning. Hence we are very happy to share portions of the transcripts from his interview here with you.

James & Chris

Chapter 1: Beginnings

My name is Tetsuhiro Hokama (外間 哲弘). The Kanji character for Hokama (外間) means outside (外) and between (間) Tetsu (哲) means Philosophy and Hiro (弘) is a combination of the bow in kanji and mu in katakana. I was born on September 14th 1944 in Taiwan. I am currently 75 years old.

When I was six years old,... I (first) learned Shuri-te from my grandfather Seiken Tokuyama. After that I move to Naha, and was taught by Seko Higa (比嘉 世幸) sensei of Goju-ryu and Shimpo Matayoshi (又吉 眞豊) sensei of Kobudo as well as by Seiko Fukuchi (福地 清幸) sensei.

When I attended Naha Commercial High School. I learned Goju-ryu karate from the instructors of the Karate Club. At that time, there were 72 members in the club, but eventually the only people who had a dojo were Ryoki Nakamura (仲村 良規) sensei of Embukan (円武館) who had a dojo on Ukishima Street, and me.

About the Dojo of Higa Seko sensei

Seko Higa was evacuated to Saipan, Tinian and other parts of the Pacific during the war. After coming back to Okinawa, Seko Higa Sensei opened a dojo in Naha city and another in Itoman town.

Later, he moved to Naha City and opened a dojo in front of Yogi's oil storage tank. Right next to the dojo, Matayoshi Shimpo Sensei built a small room where he made shamisen and taught kobudo while running his business. It was a small room with a sign that read "Okinawa Kobudo Special Headquarters" (沖縄古武道特別本部)

Seko Higa

The floor of the Dojo at that time was not such a nice floor, it was made with hammered nails and it was rough with no rubber on it. I remember that Seko Higa Sensei's dojo was quite large, which left a deep impression on me. As I recall, there were about three Makiwara standing in the room. Usually, Makiwara stood outside. In those days, the house and the dojo were often used half by half, and if it rained, practice was cancelled. Seko Higa sensei's dojo was a very fine dojo at that time. It was a tin roofed dojo, but the walls were made of concrete.

About Practice and Grade examinations

During the Sho-Dan Shinsa (Grade examinations), Yuchoku Higa (比嘉 祐直) sensei of Shorin-ryu and Nakasone Ka-Ka-/Seiyu (仲宗根 正侑) sensei of Tomari-te were at the dojo to judge us. The reason for this was that Seko Higa Sensei taught kata such as Ten-sho (転掌) and San-chin (三戦) to Seiyu Nakasone Sensei. Nakasone Sensei had learned from Grand master Chojun Miyagi (宮城 長順) Sensei as well.

Higa-sensei's dojo was a friendly dojo with such teachers, and there were always very good teachers coming to the dojo. But I was in high school at the time, so I didn't know they were such great teachers. They looked like ordinary old men. But when I started writing books and doing a lot of research, I found out later that they were great teachers.

At that time, sometimes foreigners came to the dojo. There were not many people who could speak English, so Higa sensei asked me to translate for him. Higa Sensei worked as a karate teacher at Itoman High School and then as an instructor at Okinawa Penitentiary. Higa Sensei took Fukuchi Sensei and I (an assistant instructor) went the rehabilitation facility of Okinawa Penitentiary by bus together. That was a good memory for me.

One day, the great master of kobudo, Shinken Taira (平 信賢) sensei came along with us. I wrapped Higa sensei's bag in a purple furoshiki and used an umbrella to protect it from the rain and went to the Okinawa Penitentiary with Higa Sensei and Taira Sensei. At that time, he was just coming back from Ikaho in Gunma Prefecture, Japan, and I think his right leg was a little crippled. The real name of Taira sensei was Isamu Maezato but when he came to Okinawa, he changed it to Isamu Taira.

About the schools of the time

People from many different styles were there. At the time, Higa Sensei was the president of the Okinawa Karate-do Federation. The Grade examination in those days was held in turn at A dojo, next B dojo, then C dojo, and so on. At that time, there were only four 10th dan masters of Karate. Seko Higa sensei (比嘉 世幸), Yuchoku Higa (比嘉 祐直) sensei, Shoshin Nagamine (長嶺 将真) sensei and Kanei Uechi (上地 完英) sensei.

So for example, even if you're learning Goju-ryu karate, if the chairman at that time was Uechi Sensei, you would have received a certificate of Dan in the name of Uechi-Ryu.However, if you wanted to receive a certificate from Goju-ryu, you had to retake the examination again.

About life of after war

War is a bad idea. During the war, all kinds of personalities, fine artists, karate artists, track and field athletes, and many other people died. People who were so-called "important cultural

Yuchoku Higa

Seiyu Nakasone

Shinken Taira

assets" were lost. Therefore, it is good to see culture flourish, but if it flourishes too much, there will be a war. It's a very unpleasant world.

Karate gi were not very common in those days.Do you know what an American bag is? My mother used it to sew a karate gi for me. Shoes didn't exist in those days. Bare feet were the norm. Sometimes we had lice on our heads. There were fleas flying around.

I think the masters at that time had a hard time continuing karate. They wore U.S. military uniforms and made clothes out of American bags. It was such a time. The nunchaku and Bo of kobudo were made from carriage parts.

It was that kind of time. But,in those times, each of them developed their strengths in karate.

Chapter 2: Higa, Fukushi, Nakasone

Fukuchi sensei's name is Seiko Fukuchi (福地 清幸). The Kanji character Seiko (清幸) is written as pure (清) happiness (幸).

There were a few very fortunate things that happened between me and Fukuchi Sensei.

Fukuchi Sensei was an assistant instructor of Seko Higa sensei. And Fukuchi Sensei's house was very close to my house. It was less than a five minute walk from my house in Yosemiya. Fukuchi-sensei's oldest son, Isao-san and I were in the same class.

Fukuchi Sensei had a small general store at his house and a dojo in the back of the house. Fukuchi Sensei would come home after training at Seko Higa's dojo and teach karate there. After the passing of Sekko Higa sensei, Fukuchi sensei established a dojo by himself in a place called Higashimachi. Later, he built another behind the police station in Kanzatobaru.

Seiko Higa's dojo was very large, and Fukuchi-sensei's dojo was about a quarter of that size, but there were about 20 students. We practiced there every day, and you can see from my

Seiko Fukushi

Fukushi Dojo

do-gi that everyone was covered in blood. We always used Makiwara for Tsuki, held training tools, and practiced Sanchin Ga-mi-. We practiced in many different ways. We didn't do a lot of kobudo at that school, mainly karate and Bunkai of Kata.

Fukuchi Sensei was studying the techniques taught by Seko Higa sensei, as well as deconstructing the kata that were handed down in Bubishi. At the time, many university students from the mainland (Japan) came to practice. They had been coming since the days of Seko Higa sensei. At the same time, I was the only person in the dojo who was able to go to university, and when they came from the mainland, I was more familiar with the situation on the Japanese mainland, so I often talked to them.

They didn't understand Okinawan language, so I was in charge of explaining in Japanese for them. We worked hard in a very, very small dojo. But sometimes, people would ask us to do a demonstration for visitors from the mainland. Before we went, we always ate soba. I have a picture of that.

I practiced a lot of makiwara. I didn't train a lot of makiwara now, but my hands were all black then. At that time, girls didn't really like me doing karate. When I got on the bus, I would cover my hands with a bag. Girls

didn't like it when your arms and hands were black.

About philosophy and sayings of Seiko Fukuchi sensei

Fukuchi sensei's saying is written over there (in my dojo). "Gote no sen" (後手の先) - "Take the initiative after the delay". Fukuchi sensei told us "Take the initiative after the delay"After the delay means this is not a defense. It's the first move. Take the initiative after the delay. This is the way of Seiko Fukuchi sensei "Gote no Sen". He used to say "Muchimi" - The idea is to do it softly.

Were the teachings of Higa sensei and Fukuchi sensei influenced by Bubishi ?

Only selected people could learn the Bubishi. There were some aspects that were quite dangerous to teach to amateurs, and many times it was difficult for them to understand the meaning. That's why Sensei only taught it to high ranking people. As we were high-dans, we were always with the teacher when we were in the photo.

They would only teach those people. When he taught, it was one-on-one. At the time, I was going to Yuchoku Higa sensei's dojo. Even there, the topic of the Bubishi would come up in their discussions. For example, what would

you do in this case? etc. They were talking about interpreting the Bubishi in that way. I didn't know what they were talking about at the time, but later I found out that this is what they were talking about.

Memories of Seiyu Nakasone sensei

Seiyu Nakasone (仲宗根 正侑) sensei was born in the late 1800. He passed away at the age of 94. He was born in Tomari Takahashi 1-chome. It was a wooden house at the time. Nakasone sensei was called Nakasone ka-ka-. Why Ka-ka-? Nakasone sensei would stutter ah ah uh uh when he spoke.

Nakasone sensei had taken over the (Tomari-Te) Matsumora-ha dojo. Nakasone sensei had learned from four teachers. Nashiro sensei, Kotatsu Iha sensei, Kokan Oyadomari sensei and another. Nakasone Sensei's dojo is called the Matsumora-ha Seishin Dojo (松茂良派正心道場), and the reason why it's called Seishin is because the name Seiyu (正侑) means to have a right heart. It means to act respectfully at all times. "Yanagi ni Kaze" (柳に風) was a saying of Nakasone sensei. He taught us to always respect others. However, there were not many people to take over.

How did I get involved with

Higa Dojo

Nakasone sensei? My father's name is Kentoku Hokama. Kenkotu-san was a chief carpenter. Seiyu Nakasone sensei worked with him. He used to come to my house a lot. There was a bird fighting ring in my grandfather's house at that time. They used to make the cockerels fight each other there. They would put razors on the birds and bet money on who would win. Yuchoku Higa sensei and Seiyu Nakasone Sensei often came to this house, all kinds of people came. And sometimes when the police came, we closed the door immediately. Because gambling was illegal. The ring was where we now call the Dojo Bar, right next to it. Nakasone sensei often came to the site and tried to get the birds to fight with each other.

I was fortunate to have such an opportunity to know him. He had practiced Kata of Tomari-te such as Rinkan, Wankan, Ro-hai, Passai, etc... Nakasone Sensei also learned about kobudo from Chinen Sensei of Yamani and others.

In those days, we had a martial arts demonstration at the Naha Theater. The Naha Theatre was located in what is now Kainan, near Tsuboya Street. There, various teachers such as Nakasone Seiyu Sensei, Shinjo Heitaro Sensei, Nagamine Shoshin Sensei, and Higa Yuchoku Sensei were demonstrating martial arts. Nakasone Sensei was an amazing sensei who would wrap a wire around his body and snap it off with own breathing. He was such a muscular sensei.

Nakasone sensei used to tell us to "be honest in our hearts". However, Nakasone sensei was born with a stutter that made it a little difficult for him to speak. That's why he kept repeating the same words over and over again. I think he had a lot more to say. So it was difficult for me to communicate with him. He lived a very long life and was a wonderful sensei. His karate kata was very fast.

Did you learn any Kata of Tomari-te from Nakasone Sensei?

It's not so much that I learned from Nakasone sensei. I was shown the performance at my grandfather's house. I was shown many things, but I did not learn it for a long period of time. However, I was often shown his demonstration on the tatami at my grandfather's house. I received a lot of essence from Nakasone sensei in this way.

In our next article Hokama sensei tells the story of how he came to establish Okinawa's first Karate Museum and his discovery and decoding of the mysterious and secret "bible of karate", The Bubishi.

View the complete video interview on www.bujin.tv (search "hokama")

Contact Hokama sensei via www.facebook.com/kenshikai.association

Author Information
Author
Style
email
website

Zensekai Karate Kobujitsu Renmei

Founded by Hanshi Greg Lindquist to continue the Legacy of Taika Oyata's Life Protection Art

Oyakata Kobujitsu

A sub organization within ZKKR that focuses on the Kobujitsu (ancient weapons) portion of the Oyata Legacy

Taika Oyata

Real world

Life Protection Art

Handed down to Hanshi Lindquist by Taika Oyata from 1968 until Taika's passing in 2012.

The only living person certified directly by Taika Oyata specifying that Hanshi Lindquist has the right to give rank in Taika's Life Protection Art.

Hanshi Lindquist

⇒ **Weekly Virtual Training due to the pandemic**

⇒ **Virtual Seminars**

⇒ **In person classes and seminars will resume when appropriate**

Apply now for individual or dojo memberships in ZKKR or Oyakata Kobujitsu!

L-R Renshi Agosto, Kyoshi Wuenstel, Hanshi Lindquist, Renshi Cave—Okinawa

zkkrkarate.com   oyakatakobujitsu.com   Contact: glenn@zkkrkarate.com

Kesa Giri from left to right performed by
Hataya Sensei. Andorra 2012

TOYAMA RYU IAIDO
The last loyal ones

By Sergio Hernández Beltrán
Spanish Branch Director of the Zen Nihon Toyama-Ryu Iaido Renmei

Kumitachi of the Toyama-Ryu style where Hataya Sensei performs the function of Uchi Tachi (the one who attacks), and his partner that of Shitachi (the one who is attacked).

Machida city (町田市—Machida-shi) is located in the Tokyo Prefecture, Honshu, Japan, 18 miles southwest of the bustling Grand Tokyo, and 13 miles from Yokohama. It belongs to the group of cities that make up the area known as Western Tokyo that host the homes of many Tokyo-area workers. Bordering Kanagawa Prefecture, Machida is an industrial and commercial city mainly engaged in the sale of materials for the manufacturing of machines as well as other technologies.

Getting to Machida by bus from Haneda International Airport takes about an hour and twenty minutes. From there, in ten more minutes through narrow medieval streets, you can be transported to the past, the dream of many serious practitioners of the Japanese sword. On the ground floor, at street level of a three-story building, can be found the shop / workshop in which Yoshitoki Hataya Sensei exercises his trade of Togishi (polisher). Stepping into the shop is a journey into the past of

feudal Japan. Hundreds of swords, some of them centuries old, as well as modern practice swords mix with other ancient weapons. It is a gathering point for collectors, modern practitioners of the Samurai arts, and pupils of the Toyama-Ryu style.

In the same building, climbing a narrow exterior staircase up to the third floor, you get to the Honbu Dojo (headquarters dojo) of the Zen Nihon Toyama-Ryu Iaido Renmei. When we get to this place, we are surprised by its small size. There are no changing rooms or a reception area; that is, you enter directly from the street into a small training room of not more than 40 square meters. On the other hand, this is a very common thing in most of the private, traditional dojo of Japan.

This dojo is the headquarters of the Toyama-Ryu and the place where the pupils of the school keep alive the honor of perpetuating faithfully the arts of the Japanese sword, as inheritors of the swordsmanship of Japanese Imperial Army officers of the Twentieth Century.

In the 12th year of the Heisei Period (2000), Yoshitoki Hataya Sensei was elected by his peers to become president of the ZNTIR. Currently 67 years of age, Hataya Sensei is devoted body and soul to spread the legacy of the style. "I deeply believe that the Japanese soul is tied to the sword," says Hataya Sensei. "The origin of our culture is to be found in the Bujutsu. This is what we teach and of which we feel proud."

Dojo members meet three times a week, after their working hours. By about 8:00 p.m., there can be seen people arriving by the street, wearing a keikogi (training uniform) or a traditional kimono, carrying long shoulder bags that contain their swords. The ritual in the dojo begins: after changing clothes in a corner, or in a small warehouse on the second floor, all are ready to work Taisho (scheduled gymnastics), followed by ritual greetings to the Kamiza, where a beautiful, large Shinto-style Kamidana stands out. After checking the safety of the weapons, students perform Happo-giri (eight basic cuts), with ten repetitions. In so little physical space accuracy and safety must prevail at all times, as the swords are real.

"The sword is used assuming that there is an enemy in front of us" Hataya Sensei often says. "With this in mind, I prefer to move away from concepts such as 'beauty' or 'ostentation,' and see it as a real combat. The purpose of Toyama-Ryu is the real combat kata." That fact is reflected in the next phase of the class. All students make up a human chain from the roof of the building to the dojo

Master Hataya Yoshitoki is 9th Dan Hanshi of the Iai-Do Toyama-Ryu, and Kaichoo (President) of the Zen Nihon Toyama-Ryu Iaido Renmei, in addition to being 8th Dan Kyoshi in Kodachi-Goshindo Renmei. He is also a senior practitioner of the Jiki Shinkage-Ryu Naginata style and Takeda-Ryu Yabusame (Archery on horseback).

"Samurai warriors used Iai (unsheathing and cutting in a single movement) to win their combats. They trained themselves in Tameshigiri to have a good body position and a good alignment of the sword, without which it's impossible to carry out a good cut."

and pass from hand to hand the white goza rolls (tatami mats of plaited rice straw), that have been kept submerged in drums with water for at least 48 hours to acquire a consistency similar to that of the human body.

Once stacked and placed on wooden supports to hold the rolls, everybody sits

Photograph of Tameshigiri (cut on a straw target with Gunto), by a soldier with combat gear and steel helmet of the model 90 (Tetsukabuto). The characteristic of this picture is that the soldier is executing Migi Kesa-Giri, a cut that falls at the right.

around and, on a rotating basis, each one of them, whatever his level and experience, performs his prescribed cuts. Veterans correct the younger ones. Attention and dynamic security are always kept to the maximum, to prevent the occurrence of accidents with the sharpened katana blades. Long wooden planks protect the Shinto altar, as well as the windows and walls of the dojo, to avoid any possible breakage. The atmosphere is enthusiastic and solemn at the same time.

"The Edo Period samurai warriors used the Iai forms as a method to beat their opponents in combat," explains Hataya Sensei. "This was the study of the methodology of the sword. From that point, they practiced tameshigiri (test-cutting) and methods for aligning the blade. The blade cuts if it hits straight but it will not cut anything if it's not properly aligned, so, the important thing in tameshigiri is the method of

Entrance arch to the *Toyama* Army School. (*Rikugun Toyama Gakko*).

aligning the cut. This is something that cannot be learned without practicing tameshigiri."

By 10:30, the stacked tatami have disappeared. The students of lower ranks must clean the dojo with brooms and wet wipes. Meanwhile, veterans have green tea and chat gaily in a relaxed way. Once the polished parquet flooring again appears impeccable, everyone sits with bales of tatami, which they roll up and tie in order to be soaked for use at the next cutting practice session.

"Practice should be a pleasure," insists Hataya Sensei. "Friendly relations are essential, among us as well as with people who want to discover the Japanese culture and history. We have a duty to show what our ancestors built, and transmit it to the next generation."

Around 11:00, veteran practitioners return home. However, Hataya Sensei is always ready for combat, which is a great example.

Youth with renewed energy and gallant practitioners keep arriving to the dojo. They come to practice Gekken. Gekken is a combat practice with padded swords. It's not a sport or anything created for children. Padded swords are rigid and thus they can be used to block properly. This can cause a Gekken match to be pretty severe. At a more advanced level, heavy armor and blunt steel swords are used in the

finals of Gekken tournaments in Japan. Mitsuo Hataya Sensei describes Gekken as "the study of the truth and falsehood in fencing."

In Toyama-Ryu three elements are practiced: Kata, Gekken (combat) and Tameshigiri. Samurai warriors used Iai (unsheathing and cutting in a single movement) to win their combats. They trained themselves in tameshigiri to have a good body position and a good alignment of the sword, without which it's impossible to carry out a good cut. Ultimately, they trained in Kenjutsu to learn the reality of combat. The three elements make up one.

The Toyama-Ryu Iaido is based on the Gunto Soho, the sword teaching method of the Imperial Army Toyama Academy.

The Rikugun Toyama-Gakko

The Toyama Army Academy (Rikugun Toyama Gakko—陸軍戸山学校) was established in the sixth year of the Meiji Period (明治 時代—1873), in the village ruins of the Owari clan, in the current Toyama Park in the Shinjuku Ward of Tokyo, and remained there until 1937, when it was moved 40 kilometers south-west, near the city of Zama (座間). At the end of World War II, Toyama Academy was renamed Camp Zama, (キャンプ座間) and became a detachment of the United States Army during the occupation of Japan.

The Academy trained Army officers

Excerpted from the *Gunto no Soho* manual, where appears a cadet in white uniform and armed with a *Gunto* model 98. In this case, executing the *kata*.

Photograph of an officer in full combat uniform and a steel helmet model 90 (Tetsukabuto), executing Hidari Kesa Giri with his Gunto

and non-commissioned officers in marksmanship, physical training, hand-to-hand combat, and swordplay. It also dealt with the training of musicians for military bands. Since its inception in 1873, the purpose of the Toyama Army Academy was to ensure the Japanese Imperial Army reached as soon as possible the same level as Western armies. To achieve this goal, the Academy invited French army officers who were commissioned to provide the necessary, comprehensive military training to the Japanese army officers that would form the basis of each regiment, and who, in turn, would spread throughout the entire Army the knowledge they had acquired.

3-14-14 Haramachida, Machida, Tokyo. The ground floor of the building lodges the Token Hataya Shop; the Honbu Dojo of the Zen Nihon Toyama-Ryu Iaido Renmei is located on the third floor.

The Toyama Academy Fencing Style

Most of the physical education techniques for the war, as practiced by the Imperial Japanese Army officers, were created in the physical training department of the Toyama Army Academy. In the beginning, the hand-to-hand combat techniques taught were based on methodologies of French origin. In the case of fencing, the sword fighter used a western-type saber that was commonly wielded with only one hand. But during the First Sino-Japanese War (1894–1895) and the Russo-Japanese War (1904–1905), the reliability of the Japanese sword, the katana, was revalued, and its spiritual side, along with the ancestral, psychological attraction it exerted over the Japanese people, were taken into account.

As the victor in these wars, the Japanese Imperial Army evolved quickly to catch up with the other world powers. During this period, the style of wielding the sword changed from one hand to two hands. In this context, during the fourth year of the Taisho Period (1915), the Toyama Army Academy began research work for a more traditional type of Japanese fencing, while developing a fully Japanese military sword to be introduced in the Army. For this purpose, they invited masters from various traditional schools of Iaijutsu (居合術) and Kenjutsu (剣術), mainly

Inside of the Honbu Dojo. Note the Shinto altar and next to it a picture of Emperor Meiji.

from the Omori-Ryu and Eishin-Ryu traditions. Between the eighth and nineth years of the Taisho Period, the Academy began research to improve close combat fighting ability and the teaching of handling the short sword or Tankenjutsu (短剣術), the bayonet removed from the rifle.

In Taisho 14 (1925), Morinaga Kiyoshi, who was First Lieutenant and director of the Kenjutsu Kenkyu Kai (剣術研究会)— Toyama Academy's Research Committee of sword technique—was commissioned to help create a practical system, Hakuei (白兵戦), in the modern use of the Japanese sword on the battlefield, in order to incorporate that as a subject of study at the academy.

On behalf of the Japanese army, he came into contact with Master Zenya

Gateway to Honbu Dojo of the Zen Nihon Toyama-Ryu Iaido Renmei. The sign reads Toyama-Ryu Honbu Dojo.

Yoshitoki Hataya Sensei as Togishi and responsible of the Token Hataya Shop

The author and the Monument to the Rikugun Toyama Gakko, in the current Toyama Park, where the Army Toyama School was located, august 2014

Representative shield of the Zen Nihon Toyama-Ryu Iaido Renmei with the kanji

Kunii (国井善弥), of the Kashima-shinryu tradition (鹿島 神 流), and Nakayama Hakudo (中山 博 道), an important master of the iaido style Muso Jikiden Eishin Ryu (無双直伝英信流) and the founder of Muso Shinden Ryu (夢想神伝流). He asked them their help in compiling a system of sword techniques that could be used on the battlefield. The result of the work of the Kenjutsu Kenkyu Kai and Nakayama Sensei was a codified system that was originally called Gunto no Soho (軍刀の操法) and consisted of five kata as tachi-waza (i.e., in sequences of movements for modern warfare, from an upright position, going forward, to the right, to the left and backward). These forms were designed similarly to those of modern iaido (居合道) created by Master Nakayama himself and were used for tameshigiri.

In Showa 15th (1940), Seiji Mochida and Goro Saimura, commissioned

Kendo (剣道) Masters of the Academy, conducted reviews of excellent techniques from classical schools, which were selected and combined to create and add two new kata, increasing the number to a total of seven. This was accomplished by deleting the 1925 version of form number five and replacing it with a new one, and adding two new forms, six and seven, officially adopting seven kata.

These kata were included in a manual published by the Kaiko-sha (a social organization of army officers), entitled Manual November 1940, Techniques and Tameshigiri with Gunto. The manuals were distributed to all army officers, ensuring the Gunto no Soho developed at the Toyama Army Academy was known by the whole of the Japanese Imperial Army.

In January 1942 (Showa 17), Hisakazu Tanaka created for the Academy a compendium entitled, Manual of Intensive Training with Gunto—Killing with Only One Blow (Tanki sokusei kyoiku gunto kunren—ichigeki hissatsu, 一撃必殺). The main goal of this intensive education was to teach use of the Gunto to persons without prior knowledge of kenjutsu. In the same year, forms of attacks with sword were incorporated.

Rykugun Toyama Gakko — Gunto Soho Seven Kata

Ipponme - Shomen No Teki
Nihonme - Uhou No Teki
Sanbonme - Sahou No Teki
Yonhonme - Kouhou No Teki
Gohonme - Zenmen Fukusuu No Teki
Ropponme - Zengo No Teki
Nanahonme - Sannin No Teki

The author of the article Sergio Hernández sensei, along with his Master Yoshitoki Hataya Sensei during his visit to Spain in 2016.

Preparation and rolling of the straw whites "wara", a confection in which absolutely all the members of the dojo participate, whatever their category.

AFTER WORLD WAR II: THE TOYAMA-RYU STYLE

After the defeat of Japan in World War II, Allied forces occupied the country and all forms of martial arts were banned. The Toyama Academy also ceased to exist and instruction in the techniques of military swordsmanship, as a form of military training, seemed to disappear. However, when the Peace Treaty was signed in 1952 (Showa 27), there was great demand on the part of many people for the resurgence of martial arts, and the arts started to reappear as Japan regained its independence. The Toyama-Ryu was created after the war by former instructors at the Toyama Army Academy, including Naonobu Uzawa, Yuki Yamaguchi, Morinaga Kiyoshi and Nakamura Taizaburo; therefore there is not a specific Soke (headmaster) of the style to whom we can refer.

In Showa 51 (1976), the Toyama-Ryu Shinko-kai (戸山流振興会) was founded. It was established by Tokutomi Tasaburo (徳富太三郎) and Nakamura Taizaburo (中村泰三郎), who had taught the Gunto Soho at the Academy. The

first president of the Toyama-Ryu Shinko-kai was Masuda Hideo, Hanshi of Kendo and Iaido by way of the All Japan Kendo Federation (Zen Nihon Kendo Renmei) and also a former instructor at the Toyama Academy. Taizaburo Nakamura Sensei, who started teaching Toyama-Ryu right after the end of the war, abolished the military style of stepping forward with the left foot, returning to the old style of advancing with the right foot, as performed in the styles of Iaido, checking details such as Zanshin (vigilance or alertness) and Chiburi (removing blood from the blade) and began to promote the new Toyama-Ryu. Nakamura Sensei also modified the original number of seven forms of the Army and added one more, Itto ryodan, to reach eight. This last form is actually a tameshigiri technique—its Japanese name means "Cut in two with a blow." Nakamura also included six sequences, Kumitachi, of preset combat (similar to those of Kendo, known as Kendo no Kata). Over time, the Toyama-Ryu Shinko-kai was renamed Zen Nihon

RYKUGUN TOYAMA GAKKO GUNTO SOHO - (7) KATA

Ipponme—Shomen No Teki

Nihonme—Uhou No Teki

Sanbonme—Sahou No Teki

Yonhonme—Kouhou No Teki

Gohonme—Zenmen Fukusuu No Teki

Ropponme—Zengo No Teki

Nanahonme—Sannin No Teki

Toyama-Ryu Iaido Renmei (全日本戸山流居合道連盟) and another organization, the Zen Nihon Batto-Do Renmei (ZNBR—全日本抜刀道連盟), was established in order to include other schools of Batto-Do (抜刀道). Although both federations worked in a parallel and interconnected way for a long time, since 2001, the Zen Nihon Batto-Do Renmei and the Zen Nihon Toyama-Ryu Iaido Renmei have worked completely independently. While the first is an organization that includes several styles of iaido, the Zen Nihon Toyama-Ryu Iaido Renmei is an organization focusing solely on the Toyama-Ryu style to ensure its heritage.

Zen Nihon Toyama-Ryu Iaido Renmei Honbu Dojo in Machida, Tokyo. August 2014. Visit of a team from the Spain Branch led by Sensei Sergio Hernández

The author at the Honbu Dojo performing Gyaku Kesa Giri

Kumitachi of the *Toyama-Ryu* style. The characteristic is that when it comes to advanced level *kenshi* (sword practitioners), the sword is sharp, that is, it is a real *katana*.

THE ZEN NIHON TOYAMA-RYU IAIDO RENMEI, TODAY

The Zen Nihon Toyama-Ryu Iaido Renmei is currently engaged in activities to widely promote martial arts and Japanese culture, through learning and training in the Toyama-Ryu Iaido style (⬛詫撹骶雍系À, not only in Japan but also abroad. Included in the activities of the organization are international exchanges of students of martial arts of Japanese origin, from countries such as the United States, China, Hong Kong, Taiwan, Spain, Venezuela and Andorra, where there are representatives of the ZNTIR.

It is customary that, throughout the year, practitioners of the school receive in their own country delegations of Japanese instructors, and/or they themselves travel to the Machida Honbu Dojo, to receive instruction and improve their technical quality.

Structurally, in August 2015, because of disloyalty and an attempt at destabilization by a small faction—who were summarily admonished, relieved of their duties and posts, and deprived of membership—an Extraordinary General Meeting of the Zen Nihon Toyama-Ryu Iaido Renmei was convened. A decision was made to cease being a NPO (Non-Profit Association/Federation, under the Japanese government) to form an organization where decision-making is done by the vote of the members. The idea of equality among the members is totally against the pyramidal structure of traditional Japanese schools, where members are not partners but students. The world of Budo is totally irreconcilable with the modern concept of linear organizations. Therefore, it has now

become a private organization and structurally doesn't depend on external factors any longer. The essence of the style is not to do proselytism, like most Japanese *Koryu*, but preserve faithfully its secular heritage.

Finally, in a statement of the current senior manager and Kaisho, Hataya Sensei, every student of the Toyama-Ryu is enjoined to learn the true spirit of Budo and maintain a sincere relationship between students and teachers. In this communiqué is clearly expressed the fervent wish that we members of the school, must practice together, with a smile.

Author information
Sergio Hernandez Beltran
ryubukan@hotmail.com
Web of Zen Nihon Iaido Renmei Toyama-Ryu
http://toyamaryuiaido.jp/
Web of Spain Branch ZNTIR
https://ryubukanonline.com/

Katate Suihei Giri (horizontal cut with one hand) by Hataya Sensei during the Taikai of Andorra in 2012.

Taika Oyata's
Kumiawase

How one student's research and development became a single Tan-Bo kata

By Gerard Senese

Taika Oyata's Introduction to Kata Training in his Video Tape Series, *Classical Okinawan Arts*:

"The basic movements of kata training are mainly used to cultivate natural body reactions as well as memorization of its sequence. However, in order to be a more efficient life protection technique, the movement of the hands and legs has to be combined with timing, speed, power, and accuracy. Lastly, the striking motion needs to be added to refine the techniques of each movement. The beauty of the movement itself is like a shining sword but with no edge on the blade. Kata becomes practical to use when the sharp, striking action is added as an edge of a blade is added in the final polishing process of sword-making."

It began as most of our conversations began...

...over sushi and some sake at my house. Taika Oyata came to my house twice a year, in June and November, to teach at my dojo and to enjoy home-made Japanese and Okinawan food prepared by my wife, Hiroko. It was 2009 when the discussion at my dinner table started on how kata might have been developed—the age-old question of the chicken or the egg—which came first, technique or kata? We briefly discussed Ryukyu dance and how that might have come before kata, but not related to technique at first; and then we talked about how the "ancient" masters must have developed their techniques in real situations. I will paraphrase Taika's answer, "...techniques were developed first, then the kata were developed so the ancient masters could remember and practice their favorite techniques and their principles of life protection." After we discussed that scenario for a while, I asked Taika about the empty-hand, *Kumiawase* drill (combining movements from different kata) that he had begun teaching. Taika had taken certain parts of our kata and combined them into a drill that looked like a kata, but Taika insisted it was only a drill for research and the analysis of moves that could lead to a better understanding of technique. I then asked him if the same idea of Kumiawase could be applied to weapons and he asked me what I meant.
I explained that I was viewing old

From Taika Oyata's Book, *Ryu Te no Michi*:

"Considering the seriousness and danger involved in the true, life protection arts for their survival, it is very unlikely that ancient warriors developed kata in such a simple manner as to allow just anybody to figure them out. I believe that, for serious protection arts, the contents of interpretation should be based on a higher level of efficiency, effectiveness, and accuracy; as well as natural and well-controlled movement."

videos of him working single Tan-Bo techniques in Jim Logue's dojo; and I started thinking of why there were no single tan-bo kata, and if some of the moves he was doing could be developed into a Kumiawase drill. I began to wonder about taking moves from Double Tan-bo, Nunchaku, Jo, and his Suburi Tan-Bo drills. His next line was vintage Taika, "Show me!" (Which meant, don't just talk about an idea; develop it and show him what your idea could be.)

So, the next day, at my dojo, I showed Taika the video of him doing the techniques, then the drill I had been developing. To my astonishment, he said, "Your idea—my technique? Okay, more practice!" He "fixed up" some movements, and asked me a lot of questions as to why I was doing certain moves, which I answered, "These moves are for me to remember this concept of how to trap an arm..." and, "This sequence is the first technique you did on the video that I want to remember and practice..."

As I developed more of the drill, I began to incorporate some "extra" moves between the actual techniques that I wanted to remember. When I showed the moves to Taika and explained what technique I was doing, I explained that the extra moves would "mis-direct" any student learning the drill as to the actual technique and asked him if the ancient kata might also follow this custom.

He answered, "Remember, I always say the moves are like the letters of the alphabet, and you can't use the moves in order from the kata for true life protection technique. So, maybe the masters 'mixed up' moves on

2008 Summer Conference in Kansas City began with the RyuTe Newsletter in which Taika wrote:

"Welcome to the 2008 RyuTe Summer Conference. When I began my training with Mr. Uhugusuku and Mr. Wakinaguri, I was taught differently than most are taught today. I wasn't taught to just memorize patterns or techniques. I was taught in such a way that I had to analyze what was being taught. I had to try to understand the concepts and principles of basic human motion and anatomy. I was given problems to solve which were often taught in an almost abstract way.

Over the course of my years in the United States, I have taught in much the same way. Although I have taught kata for memorization, I have also given concepts of how to find the techniques within the kata and how to develop natural ability. I have taught various exercises and drills that are designed to develop these natural motions that facilitate the execution of proper technique. In the last few years, I have put the training and teachings of previous years into their proper perspective. It is very important to remember all of these lessons and put these pieces together like a puzzle is put together. Karate should be natural and instinctive; it should flow easily and effectively from natural action. As you practice and learn, keep an open mind; remember the lessons of the past, and apply them to the lessons you learn in the next few days."

purpose. I wasn't there; I don't know what the masters' ideas were. This your idea, maybe okay, more research, more analyze our kata."

I left the extra moves in the sequence that could possibly mis-direct a student studying the drill, without further explanations from me as to the original intent of the sequences of moves.

Regarding the extra moves that I added, he said that kata are "books" written in the Chinese and Okinawan "body language," and since Americans did not understand that language, kata became useless to them and just an aerobic exercise. After he introduced *bunkai* (applications), some styles started to analyze and create bunkai of their own—this is where Taika mentioned that the kata

"book" was really a type of shorthand and if people were analyzing the kata "literally," following the moves in sequence; they would become "predictable" in their responses. He said the old masters would always have an advantage over their students, because of that. If the master's students left and went on their own, and tried to analyze the kata the way it appeared, and then went back to challenge the master, the student's movements would be predictable and could be countered very easily by the master.

Taika also talked about how each movement could be looked upon as a letter in the alphabet or as a "snapshot." As the letters had to be rearranged to make words, so too the movements in the kata had to be

Tanbo Techniques from Kumiawase Kata

Both these series contain a simultaneous parry/strike, leading into a trap and finishing with a choke.

Set #1

Set #2

Wrenching the Shoulder backward will drop the opponent to his knees (did not do for photo) to make the choke easier to accomplish

bugeisha Traditional

rearranged not only with movements from one kata, but with movements from others.

Regarding the movements as "snapshots," Taika said that comparing snapshots to a movie is the same as comparing the kata movements to real technique. If you only look at snapshots, you can never move naturally. There were "missing links" in kata; that's why Taika said it was a type of shorthand. The old masters knew the shorthand language used to create the kata, so they knew how to "put back in" the missing parts to create natural movements.

When I asked him, "How do we find the missing links?" Taika told me to look in the weapons kata and also the *Shiho Happo no Te* kata that Wakinaguri taught him. He said that was the "engine" that drove all the other kata.

As I continued to develop the drill, I blended different parts of other weapons kata into the new drill. Utilizing movements from our Nunchaku kata ("figure-8" movements), our Ni-Tan-Bo kata (how to move both arms simultaneously), and a drill Taika developed using a Suburi Tan-Bo (normally used in kendo to build wrist and forearm strength) that incorporated quick, forward and backward foot work. Taika developed that drill after 9/11 as he thought of defending himself in the aisle of an airplane, since he travelled around the country almost every weekend. Incorporating these different kata, drill techniques, and movements, I needed to analyze the principles behind the movements in the context of self-defense techniques. Taika said this would help develop my martial arts insight into all the kata we practiced.

The drill was about two-thirds developed when Taika passed away in June of 2012. After he passed away, I did not know whether I would continue to finish the drill. Throughout that summer and into autumn, I found myself going through all the old newsletters that contained articles by Taika and Tasshi Jim Logue, who had passed away eight months before Taika, in November of 2011.

Here's an excerpt from an article Tasshi Logue wrote regarding Kobudo:

"...A weapon is just a tool. In our everyday lives, we use tools to enhance certain manual functions. The writing of this article is an example. It could be hand-written, but the quality, speed, and accuracy of writing is greatly improved by the use of a word processor. Tools can be very complicated, or very simple. A lever is a simple tool requiring very little knowledge that can move large stones; the computer is much more complicated, requiring much more knowledge. To use tools, even simple ones, takes a certain basic knowledge that becomes a 'conscious reflex' action. Learning to type, searching the keyboard for each letter as you begin to learn; then developing the fluid action of your fingers 'flying' over the keyboard, is a learned conscious reflex.

"Kobudo weapons are no exceptions, they are tools developed by the Okinawan masters with the intent to multiply power, add reach, and provide self-protection. Weapons also add another dimension in training, as more physical effort is required to wield a weapon, strength and stamina are developed.

"To fully understand the usefulness of weapons training, it is necessary to also understand the purpose of kata.

"Kata is a way to develop 'conscious reflex' actions. Studying the movement of the weapon in your hands, and the footwork in weapons kata, and comparing it to empty hand techniques is another real value of weapons training. With a rigorous analysis, the natural movements of empty hand kata can be discovered in weapons kata and the extension of the unconscious movements and techniques from one to another are embedded in the brain for future use..."

With these words from Tasshi Logue, I knew that I could complete the drill into a Kumiawase/Kata that Jim and Taika would have appreciated. I did not work on it until October of that year, Taika's birth month. As Taika's birthday was approaching, I felt I needed to complete the drill to honor his legacy and try to pass on my little bit of "gold dust" which Taika had given me. Taika always said that he was giving all his students little bits of his knowledge, his "gold dust," and that we must hold on to it tightly (which meant work diligently and earnestly), or we would lose the knowledge as surely as "gold dust" would blow away in the wind if you held your hand open (which meant not taking your training seriously).

I incorporated a third self-defense sequence and developed an ending to the drill, which brought me back to the starting point of the drill. As most kata start and end in the same spot, I felt that I had completed all that was needed to meld my "gold dust" into a "gold nugget" which I could then safely pass on to future Taika Oyata Life-Protection practitioners.

After completing the drill, I practiced it by myself for the rest of that year before I showed my assistant instructors and started teaching them the drill in the beginning of 2013. I began by first teaching them the three self-defense techniques that I incorporated into the drill; then, I started teaching the opening sequences of the drill, which were designed to acclimate them to handling the single baton.

Footwork and *tai-sabaki* (body shifting), and movements from other weapons kata I practiced developed naturally into the drill's patterns and I felt Taika's words about natural motion coming to realization. Motions from Nunchaku, Double Tan-Bo, Jo, and even from my kendo training all came together in a flowing pattern, while incorporating three different self-defense scenarios that I learned from Taika.

In November 2019, Hanshi Greg Lindquist—the top-ranking instructor in Taika's "family" art, *Shin Shu Ho Ryu*, and the founder of *Oyakata Kobujitsu*—came to my dojo to teach. During that weekend, I demonstrated the Kumiawase for Greg, explained the three techniques embedded in the drill, and the way I developed the drill under the guidance of Taika Oyata from 2007 until his passing in 2012. Hanshi Lindquist was kind enough to ask me to teach it to the students in his two organizations. I accepted and taught the drill over Zoom in four different sessions in November and December of 2020. Angel Lemus Sensei viewed the sessions and invited me to write an article regarding the research and development of this drill. I accepted that offer also—the result is the article you just read.

As the old saying goes, "A picture is worth a thousand words." I began to write this article and I discovered the difficulties of putting actions into words. The photos are just "snapshots" of the movements in the drill, but I hope that the pictures fill some of the voids in my descriptions. If you are interested in further clarification, contact me anytime.

Author Information
Gerard Senese
nyryushukan@yahoo.com
631-698-2467
www.ryushukan.com

WANSU The First Kata

by Dr. Gustavo D. Albear, Ph.D.

A historical and technical review of Wansu kata done to determine its primacy as the first kata to enter Okinawan karate from a Chinese source.

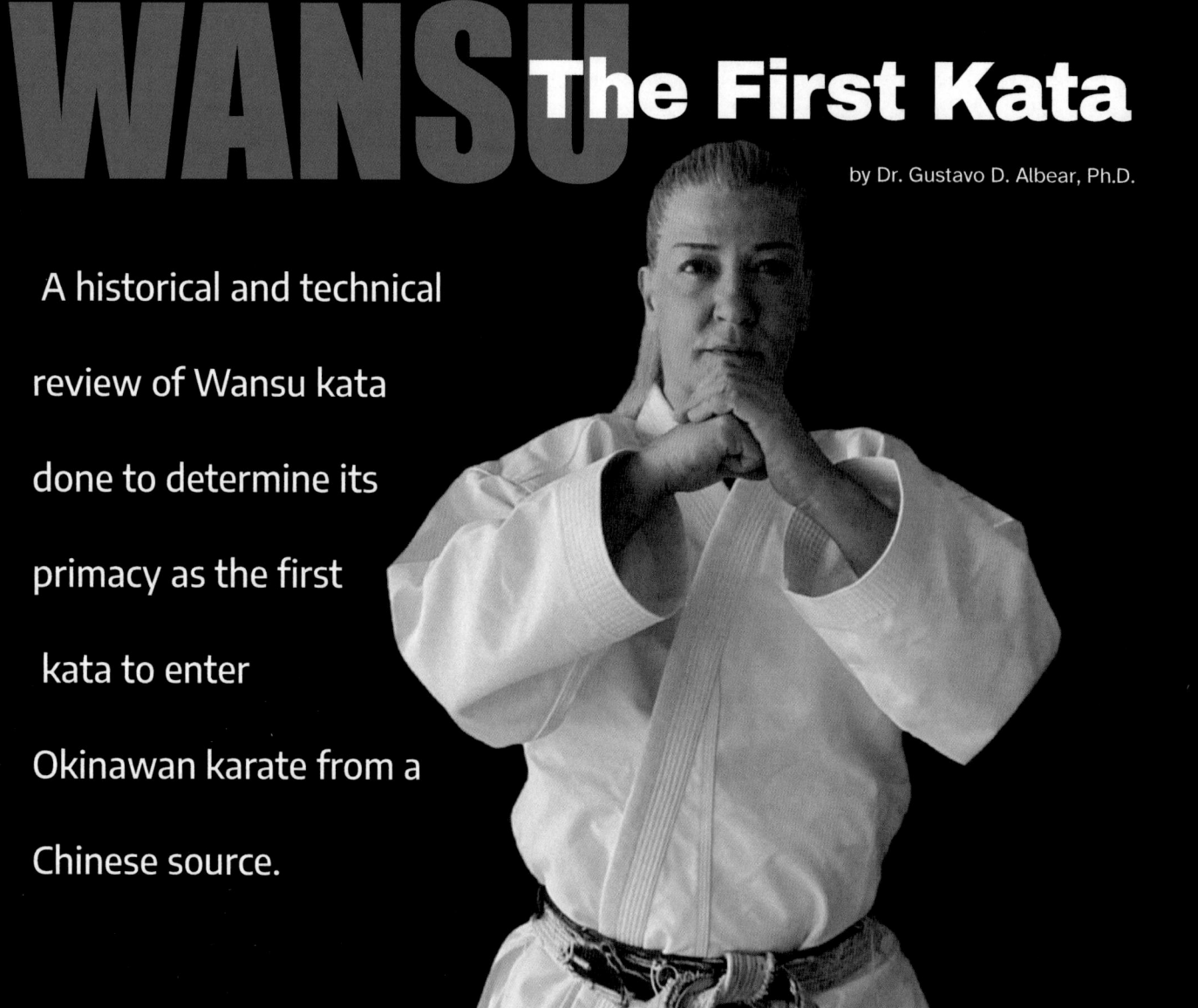

Wanshu or Wansu is an iconic kata found in two of the three major, ancestral systems of Okinawan karate, Tomari-te and Shuri-te. Specifically, the kata is part of the mokuroku, the list of katas in a style, of Shorin-ryu. It is not found in any form in the Naha-te-based systems such as Uechi-ryu or Goju-ryu. According to the oral tradition of our art, the Shuri-te-based systems pre-dated the Naha-te-based systems in entering Okinawa. Consequently, the question arises as to what was the first kata that came to or was developed in Okinawan karate, and whether Wansu could be that kata, and therefore the oldest kata that came to Okinawa from China.

There is no doubt that one of the oldest kata, if not the oldest, that can be seen across all three major ancestral systems is Seisan, a kata we discussed in our last edition. But, regardless of its multi-style membership, the question remains: Is Seisan the oldest or the first kata to come to Okinawa from China, the ancestral genesis of Okinawan karate?

Let us begin by stating the two most probable and accepted ways that katas came to Okinawa. First, we know that in the pre-style era we either have a complete kata being introduced from China by returning Okinawan nationals who had gone to China to study, or we have a series of waza (techniques) introduced by these men. Second, we are told by the oral history and to some extent by written records that sapposhi, or envoys, from China came to Okinawa with diplomatic missions and that some brought with them the Chuan-Fa or Chinese Kung-Fu systems that they studied, making this another possible way of entry into the Uchinadi, the Okinawan karate systems.

These men, some of whom are known to have stayed during their time on Okinawa in Kume village, a village mostly populated by Chinese families, visited for some time and could have taught an entire form to Okinawans who were interested in martial techniques of combat. However, the length of time that it takes to learn a method of Kung-Fu is years, not weeks or months. Having seen the Chinese systems of Chuan-Fa, one knows how complex and time-demanding they are. The sapposhi were not stationed in Okinawa for years—months was a more likely period. Therefore, the probability of a complete kata being taught by the sapposhi to Okinawans is possible if the kata was of short duration but, as a probability, their instructing the Okinawans in a long form becomes slight at best.

This points us to an alternative and more realistic approach to their teaching—waza—and shorter, reactive two-man sets of attack and defense. This method makes sense from multiple perspectives. First, the overall length of the sets fits well within the restricted learning time that the sapposhis had in Okinawa. Secondly, from a pedagogical perspective, we see that the percussive attack and defense sets are a near-perfect kinesthetic method of instruction, focusing on tactile-based learning. I say near-perfect because they cannot replace the experience of actual physical combat, but they can approximate it to a higher degree than simply performing a pattern of movements without physical contact. Therefore, waza-based, two-man sets can help the participants learn the patterns from the uke and tori relationship and aid, as a mnemonic or memory device, to generate instinctive reactive muscle memory relative to a physical act of violence. Consequently, the participants can use their contact as well as their previous training to learn and remember through touch what they might have forgotten without it. Furthermore, it is simple logic to say that two brains working on remembering a pattern are better at it than just one.

This leads us to the next question, who were these patterns taught to? Would the sapposhi have taught the Okinawan peasants their art? There

surely were more commoners than nobles. From a numbers perspective, it would be sensible, if the sapposhi wanted to increase their chances for success in having their art spread across Okinawa to teach the common man, that they would assure success by their numbers.

These techniques are found in all systems of Southern Chinese Kung Fu

Let's deal with the idea that the sapposhi would have taught the common man, the everyday man in Okinawa. And, again, as we have stated, let us look at the period with their eyes, not ours. The thought that the representatives of the Chinese government would be teaching the Okinawan commoner is just illogical. These men were nobles, and they would have only had social interaction with equals of their rank. Therefore, the students of these men would have been educated and members of the government or at least members of the upper nobility or aristocracy of Okinawa. Tode-Jutsu was not the art of the common man. It required an educated person to understand the complex connections between "BU," the martial precepts of the warriors, and "BUN," the philosophical principles of the art. Therefore, the kata would have been taught to the nobles or at least to the educated aristocracy.

One other connection of this kata being taught to the nobility comes from an insight gained through the work of historian Andreas Quast. In his

article for the online magazine and forum Ryukyu Bugei in 2015, he tells us that in the Oshima Hikki (1762), a famous record of a sea vessel of the period, the following word is used to describe the high nobility, the "Oji" or, specifically, the bloodline of the kings, the princes. The phonetic pronunciation for the word "prince," "Oji," is Wansu. As such, the logical interpretation is that the name of the kata in translation would be closer in interpretation to "The Kata of the Prince." This is not just important in determining the meaning of the kata's title but, also in understanding who was to learn and practice the techniques or the form itself.

Prior to this interpretation, there have been attempts at naming the kata based on the waza embodied in it. An example was the title, "Dragon Dumping Form." This title is based on the kata-guruma type of movement, the under or between-the-legs shoulder throw, found toward the end of the kata. However, these attempts fail to connect the name of the form itself to the supposed progenitor or provide any logical association between the name of the form and the overall techniques found in the kata. It seems that even Funakoshi Gichin Sensei, in an attempt to rename the form for the Japanese palate, tried to demonstrate this by naming the kata "Empi" with a proposed translation of "Swallow" or "Flying Swallow." It appears to this author that this evidence can be seen as a connection to an advancing jumping movement inherent in the version of the kata he learned, which is repeated a series of times within the kata. It is interesting that in his 1922 and 1925 books on Tode-jutsu, Funakoshi Sensei still uses the original name of Wansu to describe this kata, only in his later works changing the name to "Empi."

Regardless of the focus which has been put on the foundational history of Wansu kata, the fact remains that it has an oral history and a written connection to a title of the Okinawan royalty and nobility, which puts the possible historical date for the kata circa the late 1600s and early-to-mid-1700s as an introduction, vis-à-vis its title, into the Okinawan martial arts scene. As such, this connection would make Wansu kata one of the earliest karate kata mentioned in both oral and written records.

Regardless of our accepting the oral and written records dealing with the kata's primacy, we can begin to focus on more important issues that could lead us to a more precise decision relative to its genesis in our art. Consequently, the questions that we should be focusing on relative to the kata are the following:

1. What evidence exists in the waza of the kata that gives it a logical connection to its being the "first kata" to be introduced into Okinawan karate from a Chinese source?
2. Are there multiple variants of the kata?
3. If so, what can we deduce from these variations?

Looking at the first question regarding connections between the waza and Chinese-based systems of combat, we can see that the initial movement of the kata, the salutation, links its origins to China. Specifically, it links the kata to a time in Chinese history—the overthrow of the Ming dynasty by the Qin dynasty and the rebellions that tried to restore the Ming dynasty to power. During this epoch, the most famous rebel phrase associated with the restoration of the Ming to power was, "Fa Qing, Fu Ming" or "overthrow the Qing and restore the Ming." Evidence of the physical inclusion of this phrase into physical combat sets can be seen in the salutation that the rebels shared, which was a right fist positioned into a left open palm. Interestingly this salutation is the opening movement or "Yoi" preparatory posture in the Wansu kata. Variants of this salutation exist across all of the kata that bear this name, from the opening movement of all Shorin-ryu systems that include it in their mokuroku, to Ryukyu Kenpo Tode-jutsu's Wansu later renamed "Empi."

In all these systems the kanji, the Chinese character set that describes the name, for the salutation remains a constant and, as such when we look at

Ming Salutation Kyan ha

Salutation in Shotokan ryu

Manchu Salutation

the meaning of the kanji, the connectivity to the Ming dynasty and its restoration to power increases the validity of this interpretation. The character for the fist used in the salutation is "日" or "sun" while the character for the open palm is "月" or "moon." When the two characters are united, as in the physical act of the salutation the result is "日,月" which translates into one character "明," which is the kanji character for "Ming" as found in the Ming dynasty.

Interestingly, as this salutation was taught to me, the open stretched hand defined a martial salutation. This was taught to me during a seminar on Feeding Crane Kung Fu by Sifu Liu Chag-I in the late 1990s. When I made the mistake of saluting Sifu Liu with the closed left hand, he immediately came and said, "Open the hand." At that time, all I could do was to say, "Yes, Sifu," a title he requested I use with him and which I was honored to do, and to begin a search for the meaning of the left closed hand, which had been a standard in the USA relative to the salutation for years. In essence, what I discovered was that the salutation with left closed fist defined one as a supporter of the Manchu-led Qing army, while the left open hand was a true representation of the Ming dynasty.

So why then do we see many of the katas practiced in modern times that begin with a closed hand over a closed fist? One logical interpretation is that the Qing dynasty was able to maintain control over all of China and destroy the rebellion, which was focused on the land south of the Yangtze River. As such, the Manchu salutation became prevalent as a civil act of obedience to the ruling dynasty, a dynasty that lasted until the early twentieth century with its last emperor being "Henry," Pu Yi. The kata Jion, Jitte, and Jiin are all seen with this salutation and, as such, could be related to the Manchu cause or, simply said, it could be that their survival or the survival of their designer depended on their being considered acquiescent to the prevailing government rules of etiquette or acts of non-aggression towards the Qing dynasty. We will never know the answer to this question but, at least, we have a clearer understanding of the kata's salutation and its name.

Continuing with our topic, let us look at the second question we posed and determine if the variants of the Wansu kata are true variants of an original pattern or distinctly different forms. By looking at the most prevalent systems that include the kata in their mokuroku, we should be able to answer this question and, in so doing, also determine if the techniques that are demonstrated are evidential in determining connections of the waza to any systems of Chinese Kung-Fu. The two most prevalent systems that include the kata are Tomari-te systems that follow the line of Chotoku Kyan Sensei and those that follow the line of Funakoshi Gichin Sensei. Let us look at a series of techniques that are seen across the variants beyond the salutation.

The opening series on all variants deals with a low block and hook punch counter as shown below in figures 1-2.

These techniques are found in all systems of Southern Chinese Kung Fu as well as in Okinawan karate as shown in figures 3-7.

The next sequence has two variants that still have great connectivity to each other. The waza include another low block and reverse punch combination that further includes a shuto, knife-hand block or kake-uke, hooking hand block, into a sweeping block, or nagashi-uke and reverse punch combination as shown comparatively (figures 8-17).

The final sequence of the first set is demonstrative of the connection between the two main variants of the kata. These include a suriashi, or slide step, into a kosa-dachi or woman's stance in both with a gedan-barai, or low block which is seen in both variants. The exception is that, in one variant, the Shotokan method includes not a sliding step into the kosa-dachi but a jump into a kake-dachi, or hook stance, and then slides back into a reverse zenkutsu-dachi or Okinawan kokutsu-dachi with the low block, as shown in figures 18-19.

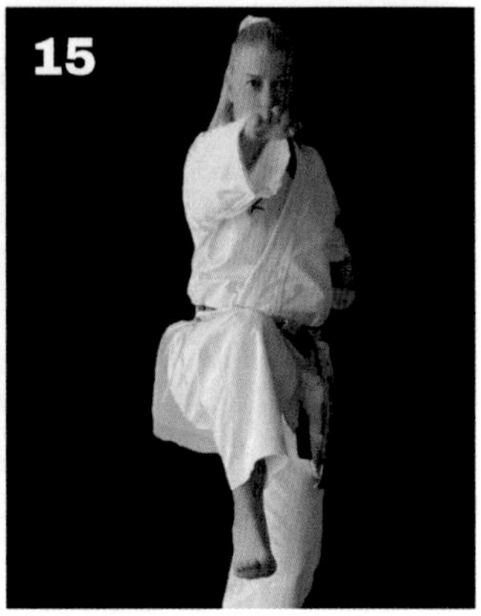

It is evident from the similarities of the two major variants that they must have a common relationship to a foundational kata. The similarities in waza only show variations due to the need of the masters who perpetuated the kata to demonstrate the adaptation of the kata to their ideas of combat. The similarities continue into the iconic move in the form which is the kata-guruma, or fireman's shoulder throw, from the hari-uke no kamae posture, or archer's block technique, which is seen in both variations. The differences in execution as mentioned above are seen in the jump done immediately after the kake-uke grab in the

Funakoshi version which is not included in the Kyan-ha versions of the kata. Both kata versions end with shuto-uchi/uke techniques further connecting the variants.

All these techniques can be found in southern Chinese boxing or Gung fu systems and even in Xing-Yi Quan or mind and fist boxing. For example, the sweeping block and punch into kake-dachi of the Shotokan version is seen in Xing-Yi boxing but with both hands open. In all southern Chinese boxing methods, the legs are seen as a foundation that allows for a focus on hands, and these two variations focus completely on solid low stances with no kicking and powerful hand

techniques. The sweeping hand in the nagashi-uke is also seen in Chinese Long Fist Boxing as a non-impacting waza. The concept of riding the arm instead of hitting the arm of the opponent is foundational to this system, as is the rotation of the fist into a punch from a chamber or hiki-te. This corkscrew punch, the traditional punch of karate, is also seen in Incense Shop Boxing as foundational, even though the hiki-te, the return of the fist to the body, does not continue completely to the side but stops almost halfway to the chamber to protect the vital points of the centerline of the defender. Further connectivity is seen in the Hung Gar system and its focus on power and low stances, evidenced in the Kyan-based version of Wansu. Therefore, quite a lot of evidence connects the variants to each other as well as to Southern Chinese Fujian Kung Fu as well as, in the case of Long Fist, Northern Chinese Kung Fu systems.

Let us now look at the third question we posed: What can we deduce from the variations of the kata? First, the variations lead us to believe that there was a foundational pattern that was

18

Kata Guruma Kyan-ha

19

Kata Guruma Shotokan ryu

changed, in the case of the two variants we are looking at, by the men who promulgated the kata in Okinawa. The Kyan version and the Funakoshi version are derivatives from the same pattern. What that pattern was that they came from is no longer available for us to see, but the techniques demonstrate the relationship to each other without any doubt. It is evident in both cases that the techniques came from a source that was closer in kihon (fundamentals) to Tomari-te than to Shuri-te. The evidence for this comes from the fact that the Funakoshi version is not in the mokuroku of the Itosu-ha systems, but exists without any doubt within Kyan-based Tomari-te systems. The Shobayashi-ryu, Seibukan, and other Tomari-te-based schools include it within their mokuroku. There are two main reasons given for the Funakoshi version being included in the Shotokan system. First, there is the probability that Funakoshi Sensei learned it from Tomari-te teachers during his time as a school teacher in that area of Okinawa. Second is the theory that he learned the kata from his main teacher Asato Sensei, and that Asato, in turn, learned it from a Tomari-te teacher. Both theories are plausible and make sense since nowhere in the Matsumura Sokon Sensei mokuroku do we find the kata.

In summary, what we see in Wanshu/Wansu is a kata that was probably introduced as either waza or short, two-man sets of attack and defense from China to the Tomari region of Okinawa and extended with repeated series of techniques into a kata. We further see from the differences between the two main variants that the individual masters who learned the kata from the original techniques devised their interpretations of the techniques for combat. Both the nature of the movements and the salutation harken back to an original system that probably was based in southern China and that arrived in Okinawa during the early-to-middle Ming dynasty. The information gained from the translation of the name and the use of the Ming martial salutation in systems such as the Seibukan school's Sukunaihayashi of Kyan Chotoku Sensei demonstrate to us this genesis for the kata. As such, we are content with a high degree of probability to say that Wanshu/Wansu was the first kata to be designed from techniques that came to Okinawa from the techniques of Chinese Kung Fu. To further validate this probability, we must turn our attention on our next article to the other iconic kata mentioned by name in the historical record, Kusanku. ✆

Sources

Behr, Edward (1987). *The Last Emperor.* Toronto: Futura

Ebrey, Patricia, (2010). *The Cambridge Illustrated History of China.* Cambridge University Press.

Funakoshi G. (1922) *Ryukyu Kenpo Karate.* Tokyo: Bukyosha.

Funakoshi G. (1925) *Rentan Goshin Karatejutsu.* Tokyo: Okura Kobundo.

History and Origin of Five Ancestors Fist: www.konghankungfu.com/ historyofngochokun.html

Keneth Pletcher, (2021) www.britannica.com/biography/Geng-Jingzhong

LFJ, (2013), from: www.kungfumagazine.com/forum/ showthread.php?65145-Chinese-Martial-Salute-Kung-Fu-Salute-Martial-Salute

Martial Arts of Southern Shaolin - An Exploration of Fujian part 1, (1877) Martial Arts of Southern Shaolin - An Exploration of Fujian part 1 - YouTube

The Martial Man, from: (1877) Long Fist Kung Fu 長拳功夫 | Master Adam Hsu | Season 3 Episode 2 - YouTube

Quast, A., (2015), Wanshū, Wansu, and Wang Ji, Ryukyu Bugei: https://ryukyu-bugei.com/?p=4675

"The Qing Dynasty," Wikipedia, from: https://en.wikipedia.org/wiki/ Qing_dynasty

Shimabuku, Z. and Smith, D. (2012), Shorin Ryu Seibukan: Kyan's Karate, Coal Mountain Productions.

Waley-Cohen, Joanna (2006). The culture of war in China: Empire and the military under the Qing dynasty.

What is Hung Gar Kung Fu & its Functional Principles, (1877) What Is Hung Gar Kung Fu & Its Functional Principles 洪拳攻防理论 - YouTube

Author Information
Dr. G. D. Albear, Ph.D. Student of Karate gdalbear18@gmail.com

The author has a Ph. D. in Education with a specialization in Teaching and Learning Sciences from Indiana State University. Dr. Albear is a 7th-degree blackbelt in Goju-ryu, a 5th-degree blackbelt in Matsumura Seito Shorin-ryu, and a 4th-degree blackbelt in Okinawan Kobudo. His book "The Mind and The Fist" is available from Peechoo Publishers.

Hiding in Plain Sight

By Chris Thomas

The "Lost" Weapons Kata of Kobu-jitsu

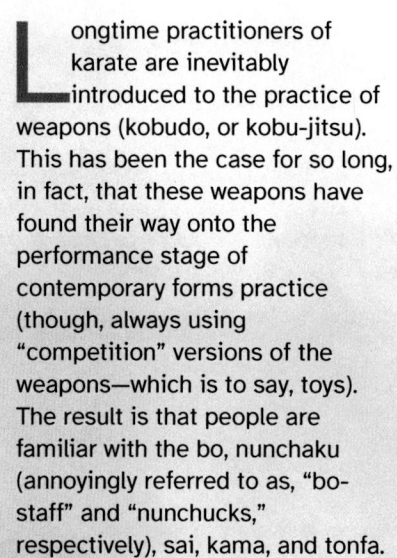

Longtime practitioners of karate are inevitably introduced to the practice of weapons (kobudo, or kobu-jitsu). This has been the case for so long, in fact, that these weapons have found their way onto the performance stage of contemporary forms practice (though, always using "competition" versions of the weapons—which is to say, toys). The result is that people are familiar with the bo, nunchaku (annoyingly referred to as, "bo-staff" and "nunchucks," respectively), sai, kama, and tonfa.

In the Standard Grip Change, the lead hand is turned over, then, the rear hand is turned over (becoming the lead hand). This method treats both ends of the bo as equal.

Those who delve deeply into the weapons arts, however, learn that there are many other weapons as well. Those interested in authentic practice understand that such knowledge has historically been transmitted via kata. But many weapons seem to lack such kata. Where is the kata for chogama (long kama—essentially a machete on a staff)? Where is the kata for the rake, the shovel or the agricultural flail? Because of these missing areas of transmission, the 20th century saw the development of kata for some weapons that had none. So, kata were developed for the nunchaku, the kuwa (hoe), and the nunti-bo to fill the void.

But is it possible that classical kata for some of these weapons are, in fact, extant? Is it possible that we have been overlooking them because they have been hiding in plain sight?

The Isshin-ryu system of karate, like many of the ryuha organized in the 20th century, has a kobudo component, consisting of sai and bo (and sometimes tonfa). The three bo kata are Tokumine-no-kun, Urashi-no-kun and Shishi-no-kun-dai. (Note: Tokumine-no-kun is actually Chatanyara-no-kun. It is likely that, in transmission, the kata was incorrectly labeled Tokumine-no-kun—an altogether different bo kata—and the name stuck.)

As an Isshin-ryu practitioner myself, I naturally practiced these bo kata. And I noticed one characteristic of Shishi-no-kun-dai which set it apart from the other two—the manner of the grip change. In both Tokumine-no-kun and Urashi-no-kun, the standard grip change is used. This means to change the grip on the bo from right side to

left side by simply to turning the hands over. In other words, the standard grip change treats the bo as if both ends of the staff are the identical.But, in Shishi-no-kun-dai, the manner of grip change is a sliding, end-to-end transition which always results in one end of the bo being forward. This means both ends of the weapon are treated as unequal. When I first learned the form, I didn't think about this. But one day, in the late 1980s (if memory serves), I asked myself, "What is different about that end of the bo?"

As I considered Okinawan kobudo weapons that are different on one end, the nunti-bo came to mind. So, I began to perform the kata while imagining I had a nunti-bo in hand. The result was disturbing—disturbing enough that I immediately bought a

In the End-to-End Grip Change, the rear hand releases from the weapon and raised up to receive the "business end" of the weapon. The other hand then slides down the shaft to take the place of the rear hand. This method is used for weapons with a front-end and a butt-end.

nunti-bo. Then, when I was able to perform the kata with the actual weapon in hand, I was struck with an immediate sense of recognition.

It is difficult to explain this moment, but I will try. I saw, simultaneously, what the moves of the kata were for, what the proper way to handle the nunti-bo was, and what nuances I was missing in how I had always done the kata.

And, I felt a bit queasy. I felt queasy because I saw that the nunti-bo isn't about catching swords with the tine (as I had often seen); it was about tearing into flesh with the hook. Nunti-bo is what any true weapon is: A brutal and nasty tool for a brutal and nasty business.

Ever since that moment, I have done this kata as a nunti-bo kata, and never again as a bo kata. And, when I have shown this to other Isshin-ryu practitioners, not surprisingly, they ended up following suit.

In Shishi-no-kun-dai, there is an iconic movement which makes my observation absolutely clear. The movement begins with a stepping strike delivered on the diagonal. This strike is immediately followed by a distinctive scooping movement—the weapon is pulled back and down, then swung up in a rising, thrusting action. Performed with the bo, it makes little sense. Performed with the nunti-bo, the meaning is self-evident.

The initial strike is aimed at the head, with the expectation that the

This notable sequence from Shishi-no-kun-dai—strike to the head, scoop down, thrust—seems useless with the bo because it is a movement for nunti-bo. The strike to the head draws the opponent's block. The downward scoop hooks and pulls the opponent's weapon, disarming him and drawing him into the finishing thrust.

The Underarm Side Strike follows an arcing path which takes advantage of the nunti-bo's unique shape by hitting with the wooden shaft and continuing the arc to pull the back-facing *yoku* into the opponent's body.

opponent will raise his weapon (a bo or some other polearm) to block the strike on the shaft between his hands. The attack from the diagonal indicates that one is attacking from his open side, which increases confidence that this response will be provoked. The instant the two weapons connect, the nunti-bo is pulled back and down. The hook perfectly catches the opponent's bo, and the pull yanks it from their grasp. Without hesitation, this is followed by a thrust with the tip of the nunti. In this way, a goofy bo maneuver is transformed into an undeniably effective nunti-bo technique.

Elsewhere within Shishi-no-kun-dai (in fact, within many bo kata) is the underarm side strike. This is a difficult movement to explain. To move the bo into this position looks cool, but it is slow and tactically inadvisable, especially when the other end of the weapon could more easily be brought to bear. The only thing that could make sense of the underarm side strike would be if the extra time required was compensated by a big effect—a big effect that would occur if one end of the weapon were truly the "business end."

When this strike is looked at from the perspective of nunti-bo application, it becomes entirely comprehensible—perfectly suited for the nunti-bo's unique shape. Consider the pathway of a bo when performing this underarm side strike. The first impression is that it is striking directly to the side. Actually, the weapon is moving in an arc, and, toward the conclusion of the blow, as the body is turning to face forward, that arc is curving backward. The nunti-bo, interestingly, has a hook which is ideally suited for such an arcing movement. When the underarm side strike is performed with the nunti-bo, the weapon impacts the opponent on the wooden shaft just behind the metal nunti head. As the arc completes, the hook is pulled into the opponent's body.

Another characteristic of Shishi-no-kun-dai are movements that involve simply standing up with the feet together. These movements are performed while pulling or hooking the weapon. With the bo, these have no purpose, but with the nunti-bo, the movements are consistently devastating. The key is to understand that the standing movement is always preceded by some form of strike. Like the underarm side strike, the blow is delivered with the wooden portion of the weapon. Then the hook is pulled sharply into the opponent's body as the entire body-weight shifts back, until the feet have come together.

Shishi-no-kun-dai, when performed with nunti-bo, fits perfectly, teaches proper use of the nunti-bo, and reveals the nuances of movement within the techniques, nuances which the architecture of the nunti-bo capitalizes upon. To be absolutely clear: I am making the case that Shishi-no-kun-dai was never a bo kata, and that it is specifically a nunti-bo form. And this means we have had a classical nunti-bo kata right in front of us. We just didn't see it.

Author Information: Chris Thomas is frequent contributor to martial arts publications around the world, a renowned instructor of *kyusho-jitsu* (pressure point fighting methods), the co-author with George Dillman of the definitive books on that subject, and a student of martial arts for over 50 years.
Assisting in the Photos: Chris Martingilio is a senior master instructor of Ryukyu kempo and taijiquan and the owner of Martingilio Martial Arts and Fitness in Madison, Wisconsin.
www.kjk-karate.com

In Shishi-no-kun-dai a strike is followed by a pulling movement as the feet come together. As a bo technique this seems to be an empty gesture. But, interpreted as a nunti-bo technique, it is devastating. The blow hits with the shaft of the weapon. The pulling movement hooks the nunti into the opponent's body, as the movement of the entire body pulls him forward and down (obviously, this is only indicated in these images).

KAKEDAMESHI

Bridging Kata and Kumite

By Noah Legel

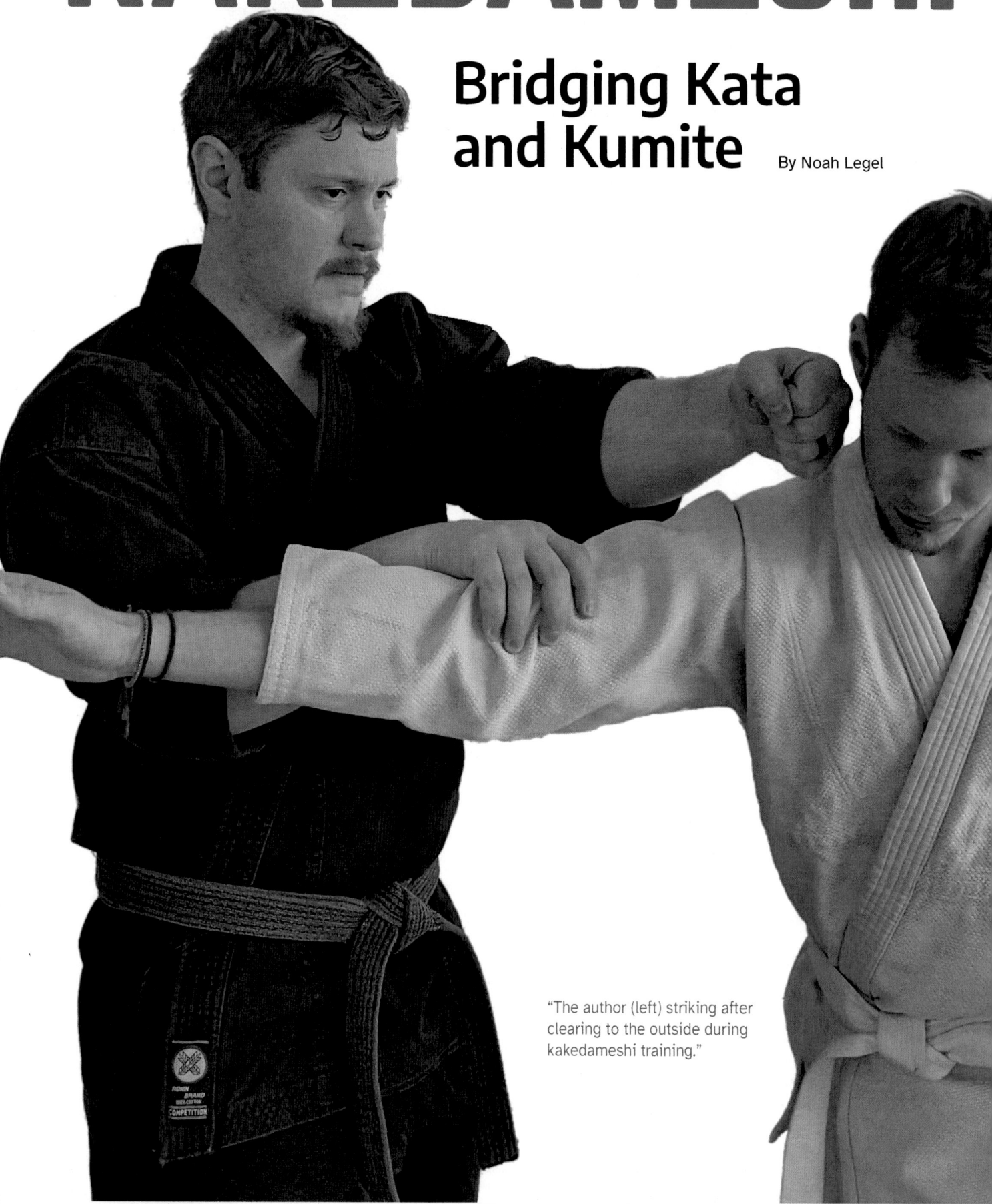

"The author (left) striking after clearing to the outside during kakedameshi training."

In addition to arm techniques, kicks, knee strikes, and foot sweeps can be incorporated into *kakedameshi*.

These days, most martial artists have a fairly consistent idea of what sparring is, and even though different arts and styles will use a variety of rulesets, most will still recognize the practice of sparring. For karateka—those who study karate—the most popular approach to sparring (kumite) is the point-fighting system, wherein two competitors attempt to land the first clean strike in order to earn points, and the competitors are reset every time a point is scored, or a penalty called. While many karateka train for this type of sparring, and enjoy competing in tournaments under these rulesets, most of them will be quick to point out the obvious disconnect between their sparring and the kata that they practice. Despite this, karateka are constantly told that kata is the foundation of karate, and vital to the proper development of the fighting skills of the Okinawan people. So, how did this disconnect come to pass, and how do we bridge the gap?

When karate was transplanted from Okinawa to the Japanese mainland, it was promoted as a method of physical and personal development, following the tenets of Japanese budo culture. As such, it became popular with athletic young men, particularly those of college age, and clubs began to spring up in schools and universities. Young men, traditionally being prone to bouts of machismo, often like to compete against each other in their chosen physical pursuits. Karate was no different. In October of 1957, the Japan Karate Association hosted the 1st All Japan Karate Championship in Tokyo, and it was the first officially recognized tournament to feature the point-fighting ruleset that karate is now known for.

Prior to this, many organizations were experimenting with different ways of approaching the idea of competitive sparring, in order to pressure-test the fighting methods of karate in the modern world, while simultaneously drawing attention through competitions, which could be easily promoted to the public in order to spread the art. Many Japanese karateka took inspiration from the competition ruleset of kendo—which was already widely popular in Japan—and developed sparring methods based on the ideals of kendo. This led to the long-distance, first-strike-focused sparring that evolved into the point-fighting rulesets we know today. The intentions were good, but some of the true essence of Okinawan karate was lost in translation.

The fighting arts of Okinawa, at their core, are meant for fighting at close range, and this is the type of fighting that the classical kata were built to represent. Of course, this type of fighting incorporates standing grappling techniques, throws, chokes, and joint locks, in conjunction with strikes. Funakoshi Gichin, the founder of Shotokan and the father of Japanese karate, omitted much of this material from his system in order to avoid competing with the native fighting arts of Japan, such as Sumo, Judo, and jujutsu. This was necessary to promote karate, as Japanese culture at the time was strongly nationalistic, and tended to view Japanese arts, sciences, and practices as being superior to all others. Unfortunately, this likely left many karateka in Japan with an incomplete idea of what the techniques of karate were for, which became evident in the kihon (basic) techniques that are now staples of point-fighting. Indeed, this was pointed out by Mabuni Kenwa (founder of Shito-Ryu), who one wrote that, "the karate that has been introduced to Tokyo is actually just a part of the whole. The fact that those who have learnt karate there feel it only consists of kicks and punches, and that throws and locks are only to be found in Judo or jujutsu, can only be put down to a lack of understanding."

This type of competition fighting actually became widely successful, especially as occupying Allied forces brought karate back to their home nations after World War II. It became so successful, in fact, that karateka in the heartland of karate—Okinawa itself—eventually joined in. Some, such as Mabuni Kenwa and Nakamura Shigeru (the founder of Okinawan kenpo), promoted bogu kumite (armored sparring) in an attempt to provide a safe method of sparring with the real fighting techniques of karate. Unfortunately, the armor was bulky, restricting some of the techniques that the wearer could perform, and didn't adequately protect against some techniques, so sparring still had to be adjusted. In the end, the sparring methods of Japan won the popularity contest, although some schools still utilize bogu kumite.

For the better part of the last century, the development of sparring for karateka has been focused on the point-fighting method, and there are highly skilled, very athletic competitors all over the world who prove the effectiveness of their skills in the ring on a constant basis. If we look back far enough in the history of karate, however, we can see that effectiveness used to be tested in very different ways. We know from accounts of Motobu Choki's youth that he actively visited the red-light district of Tsuji to get into fights in order to test his abilities, and other karate masters, such as Kyan Chotoku, advocated visiting such places, which would undoubtedly lead to the occasional violent encounter. There was also crime, of course, and gangs of youths who would attack people in the streets, which provided additional, real-life pressure tests. None of these are training methods, however. For that, we have to look at the formal challenge matches of karate, and how karateka trained for them— kakedameshi.

The word kakedameshi can be translated in a variety of ways, but the simplest meaning would be "hooked testing." In this case, "hooked" is meant to reflect the idea of participants connecting to each other. Another word for this practice is kakete, or kakidi in Uchinaaguchi (the native Okinawan language), which literally means "hooked hands." This may seem like a rather abstract idea, but remnants of these practices can

A student practices a takedown from *Naihanchi Shodan* in *kakedameshi*

"The fighting arts of Okinawa, at their core, are meant for fighting at close range, and this is the type of fighting that the classical kata were built to represent."

still be seen in the kakie exercises that are still popular in Goju-Ryu, Uechi-Ryu, and some schools of Shorin-Ryu, which make the name a little clearer. Motobu-Ryu Udundi (Palace Hand) also regularly incorporates kakidi training, which, according to Motobu Naoki, was the standard method of sparring and developing fighting skills when the style was being developed.

While descriptions of the original practice of kakedameshi are rather sparse, and often incorrect— suggesting that kakedameshi was the name for getting into street fights and barroom brawls—the editor's notes of Nagamine Shoshin's book, Tales of Okinawa's Great Masters, provides a

fairly clear definition. Those notes say that it is "a very aggressive version of taiji pushing hands," where opponents try to knock each other down, use "manipulation techniques," and strike each other, including with kicks, elbows, and knee strikes. There is also a story, told by Motobu Choki, about visiting Funakoshi Gichin in Tokyo and, being unimpressed with what he saw, challenging his contemporary to kakedameshi. In that instance, he specifically noted that he thought striking Funakoshi would be excessive, and chose to throw him to the ground with a wrist lock several times, instead.

Through comments like these, we can piece together a fairly good idea of what kakedameshi might have looked like in the 19th and early 20th Century, and it looks a great deal like the clinch-work and standing grappling drills found in other traditional martial arts, like shuai jao (traditional Chinese wrestling), as well as modern practices like mixed martial arts. The most notable differences would be the use of torite/ tuidi (seizing hand techniques) to lock the joints, and kyusho/chibudi (vital point techniques) to attack particularly vulnerable targets that would be illegal in most competition formats.

This brings us back to our kata,

Three Simple Drills to Introduce Kakedameshi Principles

The following drills are intended to help students develop a foundation of skills that they will use in kakedameshi, and can be utilized by everyone from white-belts to black-belts, because the drills advance with the student. Initially, the student can simply practice their natural reactions within the context of the drill. Over time, as students learn more techniques and become more advanced, their reactions will become more refined, controlled, and effective.

1. Lead and Follow

1. Lead and Follow—This simple drill is designed primarily to develop tactile sensitivity, proprioception, and muchimidi (sticky hands), and can be done with one or both hands.
- a. Participants begin by crossing the arms at the wrists
- b. The designated Leader (black dogi) will move their arm, slowly at first, and increasing in speed over time, through all angles of movement possible.
- c. The designated Follower (white dogi) will try to keep their arm connected to the Leader's arm, no matter where it goes or how it moves.

2. Lead and Defend

2. Follow and Defend—This drill uses the same format as the Lead and Follow drill, and builds on the skills developed in it by incorporative defensive methods.
- a. Participants begin by engaging in the Lead and Follow drill
- b. The designated Leader (white dogi) attempts to push or strike the Follower (black dogi), at random
- c. The designated Follower will attempt to maintain contact with the Leader, while deflecting their attacks, or attempting to then press the Leader's arms into their body to prevent a second attack

3. Defend and Attack

3. Defend and Attack—This drill once again builds on the Lead and Follow drill, as well as the Follow and Suppress drill, and adds countermeasures to deal with an opponent's defense.

a. Participants begin by engaging in the Follow and Defend drill.

b. As the designated Follower (black dogi) defends against the designated Leader's (white dogi) attack, they should enter into striking, locking, strangling, or throwing techniques, depending on what best suits the situation

which have long been non-representative of the kumite that most karateka are familiar with. Some of the movements can be made to work at long range, certainly, but if we look at the movements in the context of close-range fighting, they become much more versatile. Simply crossing arms with a partner, as is done in kakie, and practicing uke-waza (receiving techniques)—more commonly referred to as "blocks"—will give a karateka instant feedback as to how the motions of kata can be used to manipulate an opponent at close range.

As the motions of the kata become more complex, one can begin to see how strikes, locks, and takedowns flow naturally with the limb controls used to deal with an opponent who is already within arms' reach. There is little need for the leaping oi-tsuki (lunge punch) to close the gap, because the gap isn't there to begin with. This may seem very limiting, to some, but consider the fact that most real-life, self-defense situations take place at conversation distance, or closer, and the sensibility of this training method becomes evident. It also provides karateka both with a method of developing skills, and a method of pressure testing those

skills against others who are actively fighting back, providing a gateway for further training opportunities.

The simplest way to begin incorporating kakedameshi into one's training is with kakidi or kakie drills. Some see these exercises as little more than forearm conditioning and a shoulder muscle workout, but they are actually very useful platform drills for introducing resistance to a student's technique practice. By maintaining forearm contact, both partners develop tactile sensitivity and proprioception, so that they can feel what their partner is doing, even with their eyes closed. They will know if their partner's arm is pulling, pushing, rising, sinking, or circling.

This develops an excellent foundation from which to launch into the movements of kata, which are used to control, block, or redirect the opponent's movements and allow one to launch their own attack. Through kakidi and kakie drills, this can be taught in a controlled, safe manner, where students can practice individual kata techniques focused on specific actions of the opponent. Over time, the drills can be made more active, more unpredictable, and more resistant, eventually leading to

freestyle kakedameshi practice.

To engage in kakedameshi, the key is to remain connected to your partner as much as possible. Generally, a simple starting point is for both participants to take up meotode-gamae (husband and wife hands posture), with their lead arms crossing at the wrist, in the same manner as kakidi and kakie drills. Alternatively, the participants can cross both arms at the wrist, in a posture reminiscent of the morote-chudan-uke (double middle "block") positions found in Sanchin. In either case, both participants are then allowed to freely attempt strikes, shoves, pulls, takedowns, joint locks, and chokes, as well as defending against such attacks, provided they are also attempting to control their opponent in the process.

It can be tempting to break the connection and begin simply punching away at each other, but this doesn't accurately focus on the intent of the exercise, and tends to become a war of attrition that is won by the tougher, stronger fighter, which resembles the "knockdown" style of fighting that was pioneered by Masutatsu Oyama (the founder of Kyokushin). This is an excellent way to test your fighting spirit, and is especially suited toward the young, athletic, and healthy of body. Ideally, though, our goal should be to avoid damage as much as possible, and utilize technique and skill to overcome disadvantages in size and strength, so we should try not to be dragged into such exchanges.

This isn't to say that kakedameshi training is easy. In truth, kakedameshi is difficult, tiring, painful, and allows for the practice of many dangerous techniques, making it more risky to engage in than the long-range point-fighting most karateka practice. This is part of why it became less popular over time, and as such, very few systems still utilize it, but it is precisely the type of training that traditional karate needs to get back to its roots. Traditional martial arts are often criticized for their impractical training methods and unrealistic sparring, and while part of that comes from ignorance, there is certainly some truth to it, as well. If your sparring does not reflect the skills developed in the rest of your training, then either your training is ineffective, or your sparring method doesn't accurately emulate the type of fighting your training is geared toward.

Some traditional martial artists have altered their training to suit their sparring, choosing to eschew kata practice and focus entirely on drills that build skills for competitive point-fighting. Others choose to cross-train in other martial arts, such as Brazilian Jiu-Jitsu, Sambo, or MMA, where they can engage with a resisting partner and pressure test techniques in their appropriate context. While there is value in both approaches, it is important to remember that the traditional arts we practice today came from practical fighting methods, and if we train appropriately, there is a lot of effective combative skill to be gained from them. To overlook our roots is to allow them to wither and die. ☻

Author Information
Noah Legel
azpracticalkarate@gmail.com
www.karateobsession.com

KARATE WEBINARS
with Noah Legel

Plan a private online seminar for your dojo from anywhere in the world!

KATA, BUNKAI, KUMITE, AND MORE!

Mention Bugeisha when you book before September 1st, 2021 to get 20% off

azpracticalkarate@gmail.com

ARIZONA PRACTICAL KARATE
PROTECT · BREAK FREE · TRANSCEND